DK

AN ANTHOLOGY OF

Stargazing

Look out for these icons in the book to locate different objects in the night sky.

 Brightest star

 Galaxy

 Nebula

Star cluster

AN ANTHOLOGY OF
Stargazing

Written by Abigail Beall
Illustrated by Angela Rizza and Dilbag Singh

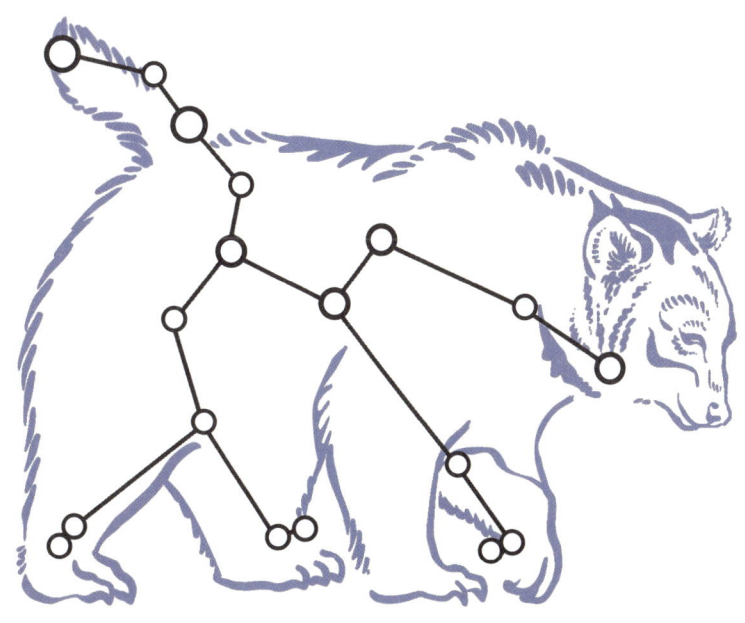

Contents

What is stargazing?......................6
In the night sky............................8
Looking at the night sky............12
Life of a star...............................14
Does the sky move?..................16
The celestial sphere..................18
What is a constellation?............20

NORTHERN CONSTELLATIONS......22
Orion...23
Andromeda...............................24
Cassiopeia................................25
Perseus.....................................26
Triangulum................................27
Auriga.......................................28
Camelopardalis........................29
Canis Minor..............................30
Leo Minor.................................31
Lynx..32
Monoceros...............................33
Boötes......................................34
Ursa Major...............................35
Canes Venatici........................36
Coma Berenices......................37
Corona Borealis......................38
Serpens...................................39
Hercules..................................40
Draco......................................41
Ursa Minor..............................42
Aquila.....................................43

Cepheus..................................44
Cygnus....................................45
Delphinus................................46
Equuleus.................................47
Asterisms................................48
Lacerta...................................50
Lyra..51
Pegasus.................................52
Sagitta...................................53
Vulpecula..............................54

SOUTHERN CONSTELLATIONS......55
Caelum..................................56
Cetus.....................................57
Lepus....................................58
Columba...............................59
Star hopping.........................60
Eridanus...............................62
Fornax..................................63
Horologium...........................64
Hydrus..................................65
Dorado.................................66
Mensa..................................67
Phoenix...............................68
Pictor...................................69
Reticulum............................70
Sculptor..............................71
Myths and legends.............72
Antlia..................................74
Canis Major.......................75

Carina	76
Chamaeleon	77
Crater	78
Hydra	79
Puppis	80
Pyxis	81
Sextans	82
Vela	83
Volans	84
Apus	85
Ara	86
Centaurus	87
Circinus	88
Corvus	89
Crux	90
Lupus	91
Musca	92
Norma	93
Triangulum Australe	94
Corona Australis	95
Grus	96
Indus	97
Microscopium	98
Piscis Austrinus	99
Pavo	100
Octans	101
Scutum	102
Telescopium	103
Tucana	104

ZODIACAL CONSTELLATIONS 105

The ecliptic	106
Capricornus	108
Aquarius	109
Pisces	110
Aries	111
Leo	112
Virgo	113
Scorpius	114
Cancer	115
Libra	116
Gemini	117
Taurus	118
Sagittarius	119
Ophiuchus	120
Stargazing tips	121
Careers in stargazing	122
Glossary	124
Index	126
Acknowledgements	128

What is stargazing?

When the Sun sets and the sky grows dark, we are treated to a spectacular view of the Universe. Looking up at the stars, planets, the Moon, and other objects in the night sky is called stargazing or amateur astronomy. People who study these objects in the night sky are called stargazers or astronomers.

Early stargazing

For centuries, humans have watched the night sky and noticed how stars twinkle, the Moon changes shape, and planets move across the sky. They used these observations to make calendars and tell time. Ancient stargazers also believed that events in the sky could predict what might happen on Earth. This idea later developed into the study of astrology.

The 6th-century Indian astronomer Varahamihira wrote an encyclopedia where he collected early ideas from western and Indian astronomy.

Ancient astronomers

The first astronomers around the world created their own stories about the night sky, especially the stars. Astronomers like Claudius Ptolemy and Zhang Heng developed the idea of a celestial sphere around the Earth, which is still used today to map space objects.

Claudius Ptolemy

Zhang Heng

Recording the stars

Ancient astronomers studied the night sky and recorded their observations in star charts and maps that continue to guide stargazers today. Early findings of astronomers like Johannes Hevelius and Nicolas Louis de Lacaille have helped modern astronomers understand the Universe in more detail. While Hevelius watched stars from his terrace, Nicolas went on an expedition to discover new groups of stars.

Hevelius's *Prodromus Astronomiae* (1690) introduced seven new constellations, including Lynx and Leo Minor.

Using the stars

For a long time, sailors have used stars to navigate at sea. They discovered that, just like the Sun helps show direction during the day, the movement of stars could guide them at night.

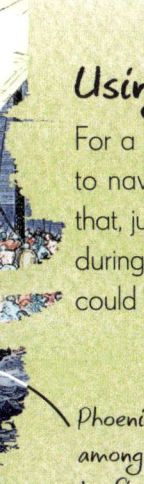

Phoenician sailors were among the first to use stars to find their way at sea.

Stars

Stars are massive balls of glowing gases, mostly hydrogen and helium, held together by gravity. These gases constantly burn inside a star to create heat and light. Countless stars are scattered across the Universe. The Sun is one of them, and it's the closest to our planet.

Earth has only one moon, but other planets have several.

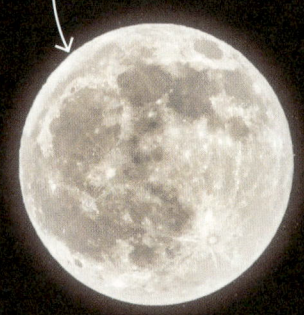

Moons

Moons are usually round objects that orbit the planets. They mostly have rough, uneven surfaces, which are sometimes visible to the naked eye. While moons don't produce light of their own, they appear to glow because they reflect light from stars.

In the night sky

The sky is a vast stretch of wonders. It's filled with millions of celestial objects — from fiery stars to icy moons. When these objects interact with one another or their surroundings, they create celestial events, such as meteor showers.

Galaxies

Enormous collections of stars, gas clouds, and dust particles are called galaxies. There are billions of galaxies in our Universe, and some can be seen by the naked eye. Galaxies come in different shapes and sizes. We live in a spiral galaxy, called the Milky Way.

A meteor is also called a shooting star as it looks like a streak of light moving across the sky.

Meteor showers

Rocks that travel through space, like asteroids, leave behind trails of dust. When these bits come close to the Earth, they burn up and create a bright flash called a meteor. As Earth moves through a patch of this space dust, we see many meteors at once. This is called a meteor shower.

Light years

One light year is the distance travelled by a beam of light in one Earth year (about 365 days). Astronomers use this to measure vast distances in space. One light year is equal to nearly 9 trillion km (6 trillion miles).

Earth

Proxima Centauri

This closest star to Earth after the Sun is 4.25 light years away, which is about 40 trillion km (25 trillion miles).

Moon's shadow on Earth

The Sun's light is blocked by the Moon.

Sun

Moon

Earth

Eclipses

Just as Earth orbits (goes around) the Sun, the Moon travels around the Earth. When all three line up and block sunlight, an eclipse occurs. A solar eclipse happens when the Moon comes between the Sun and Earth. A lunar eclipse occurs when the Earth moves between the Sun and Moon, casting its shadow on the Moon.

Constellations

There are 88 official star patterns in the night sky, known as constellations. Stargazers use them to locate stars and other celestial objects. The stars in a constellation may look close together, but they aren't necessarily near each other in space.

The Ursa Major constellation glowing in the night sky

Auroras

A dazzling dance of green, purple, and blue light fills the night skies near the Earth's poles. This is called an aurora. It occurs when the particles in sunlight interact with gases in polar surroundings, creating waves of light. Auroras are called the northern lights at the North Pole, and the southern lights at the South Pole.

North Star

Among the billions of stars in the sky, the North Star, or Polaris, is considered exceptionally important by stargazers. Sitting almost above the north celestial pole, it helps us locate constellations in the northern hemisphere.

Polaris never sets in the northern hemisphere.

Looking at the night sky

You don't always need special equipment to begin stargazing. Thousands of stars, along with several planets and galaxies, are visible to the naked eye. But if you want to explore the sky's deeper secrets, these tools can help.

Give your eyes time to adjust to the darkness, and you'll see many more stars.

Binoculars

Binoculars help you see faraway objects by making them look bigger. They're usually small and easy to carry, and can reveal amazing sights, such as the Moon, galaxies, and star clusters. Binoculars with larger lenses work better at night or in low light, but they can be heavier to hold.

Telescopes

A telescope is much bigger than binoculars. It makes distant objects appear closer and larger. Though tricky to use, it helps you see finer details of planets like Saturn's rings, and clearer views of stars, galaxies, and nebulae.

The compass needle always points in the North-South direction.

Compass

A compass shows which direction you're facing — north, east, south, or west. It works by using the Earth's magnetic field, an invisible force around the planet. The compass is quite useful while stargazing since some constellations appear in specific directions.

Apps and computers

Many apps and computer programs make stargazing easier and more fun. Some identify constellations as you point your device at the sky. Others alert you to good stargazing weather or upcoming events like auroras or meteor showers.

Computer programs can help you find where the things you want to see will appear in the sky.

Life of a star

Stars begin their lives in glowing clouds of dust and gas. Some stars live together in starry clusters, while others shine alone. As they grow, stars change in size, shape, and colour. When their time is up, they go out with a bang!

Types of star

Most stars appear as white dots in the night sky. But a closer look through a telescope reveals stars in all sorts of colours and sizes. From hot blues and cool reds to tiny dwarfs and huge supergiants, stars change throughout their lives.

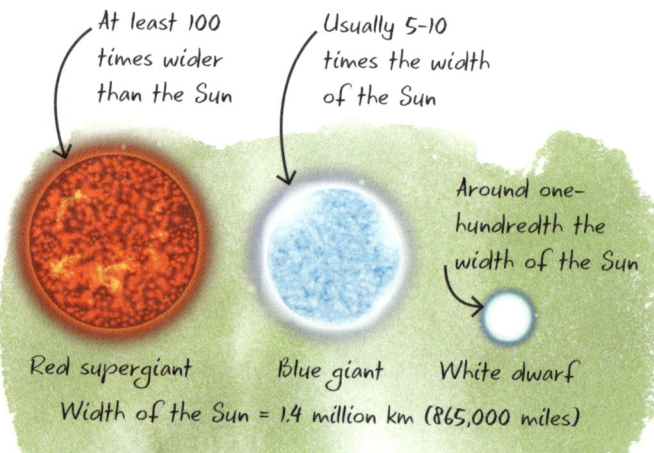

At least 100 times wider than the Sun

Usually 5-10 times the width of the Sun

Around one-hundredth the width of the Sun

Red supergiant   Blue giant   White dwarf

Width of the Sun = 1.4 million km (865,000 miles)

Born in a cloud

Stars are born in huge clouds of dust and gas called nebulae. Some nebulae form when gravity — a force that pulls things together — gathers clumps of dust and gas in space. Others come from the explosive remains of a dying star.

Living together

Sometimes a group of stars is held together by gravity and forms a huge star cluster. Open star clusters contain hundreds to thousands of loosely bound stars. Globular star clusters are larger, denser, and spherical. They hold millions of stars, and can live for billions of years.

The Pleiades in Taurus is the brightest star cluster, and it's visible to the naked eye.

The last hurrah

When a star dies, it explodes with a huge blast of light and energy called a supernova. This can also happen in a star system, where two stars orbit each other — one a white dwarf. When the bigger star runs out of fuel, the white dwarf may crash into another star and boom — another big star blast!

In an eclipsing binary system, the stars block each other's light while orbiting, creating a flickering effect.

Variable stars

Some stars are variable, meaning their brightness changes over time. Others send out pulses of light as they spin. Many variable stars belong to binary systems — where two stars, held together by gravity, orbit each other.

Does the sky move?

Well, yes and no. The sky appears to move because of the Earth's movement. As our planet spins from west to east, the stars and other celestial objects seem to travel across the sky in the same direction.

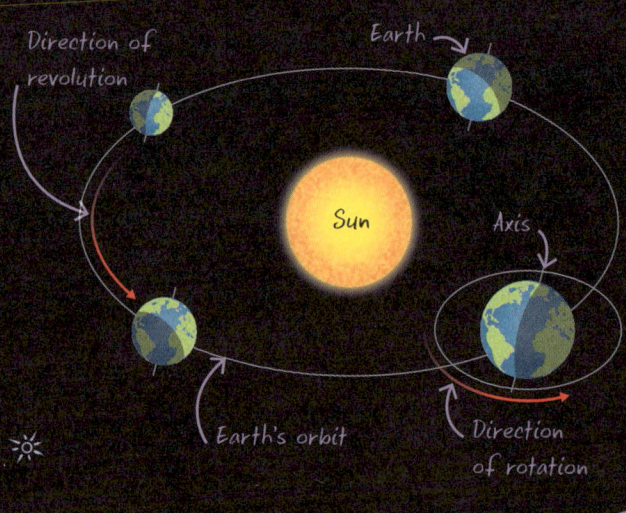

Earth's movement

The Earth revolves around the Sun, as well as spins, or rotates, on an imaginary line called an axis. The part that tilts towards the Sun experiences day. It is night on the other side. Changes in sunlight levels also lead to shifting seasons.

Moving planets

All planets in our Solar System orbit the Sun at different speeds. As the Earth moves along its own path at a particular speed, the other planets appear to drift across the sky like stars, but faster.

Star trails

While the Earth rotates, the stars appear to move across the sky, changing how the sky looks through the evening. Some stars rise and set, while others stay visible all night — but their positions seem to keep shifting. In fact a star rises about four minutes earlier each night! In the northern hemisphere, stars circle the North Star, and in the southern hemisphere, they revolve around the south celestial pole.

To capture glowing star trails, leave your camera to continuously shoot the night sky for a few hours.

Standing at the North Pole, you will see the star trails moving overhead.

When between the poles and equator, you will observe the star trails tilted to the right.

At the equator, the star trails rise from east and set in west.

Models of motion

For many years, astronomers believed in an Earth-centred model of the Universe. It was only in the 16th century that they discovered the Earth was not fixed. Instead it moves around the Sun at a constant speed.

Danish astronomer Tycho Brahe's model of the Earth-centred Universe

The starry sphere

Astronomers visualize each star in the sky as a dot of light placed on the surface of the celestial sphere. This starry sphere is concentric with Earth — meaning it has the same centre — and appears to rotate on the same axis, but in the opposite direction to the way Earth moves.

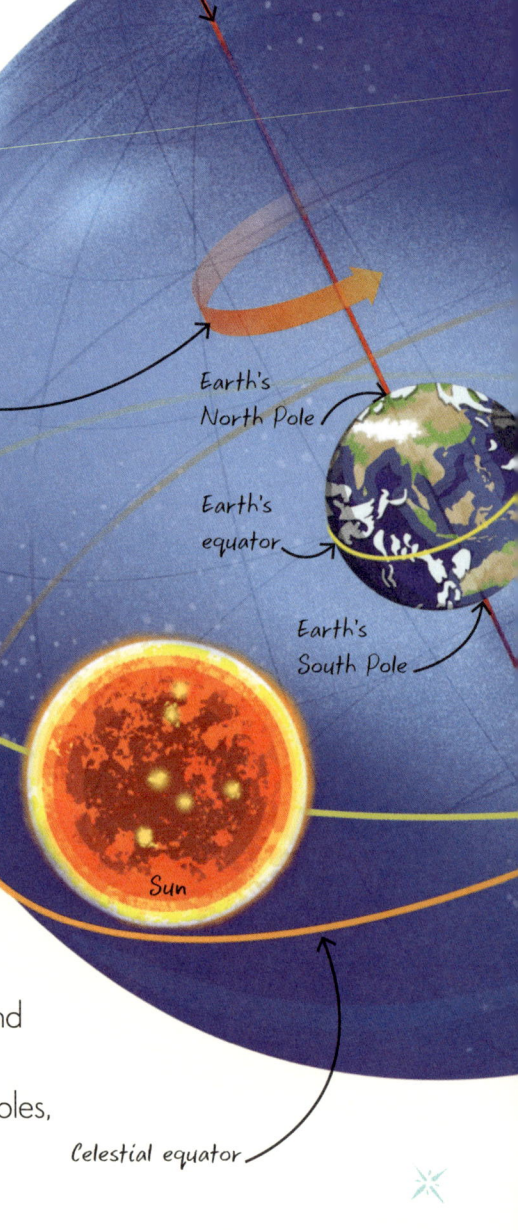

North celestial pole

Direction of Earth's rotation

The Sun's path on the celestial sphere

Earth's North Pole

Earth's equator

Earth's South Pole

Sun

Celestial equator

The celestial sphere

Our planet is surrounded by millions of stars, galaxies, and other celestial objects. To trace their locations, astronomers imagine them placed on a giant sphere around the Earth. This is called the celestial sphere. Right above Earth's poles are the celestial poles, and the celestial equator lies directly over Earth's equator.

Celestial coordinates

Like latitude and longitude on Earth, the celestial coordinates tell you the position of space objects on the celestial sphere. The first coordinate is called right ascension and is like the longitude of Earth. The other is called declination, which is the equivalent of latitude.

Right ascension, measured in hours, tells the time of appearance, while declination, measured in degrees, indicates the location.

South celestial pole

Finding stars

Flat, circular maps of the sky, called planispheres, are used to locate stars, constellations, and other sky objects. Due to the movement of Earth, stars and planets appear at different positions in the sky, depending on the time of the day and year. You can rotate a planisphere to see what the sky looks like at a particular time.

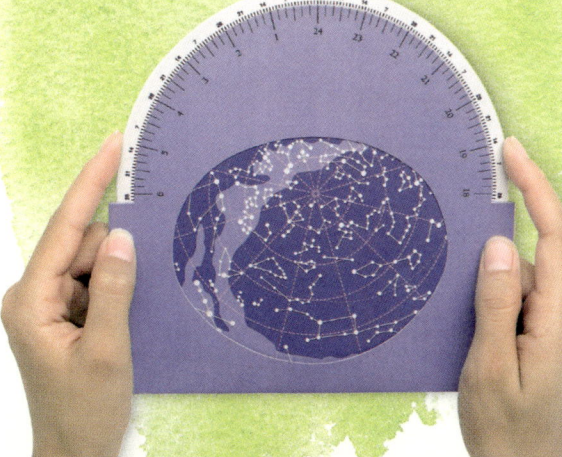

What is a constellation?

A constellation is a group of stars that form a pattern. Early astronomers identified many star patterns and named them after the shapes they saw. Today, there are 88 officially recognized constellations, each with its own name and features.

Recording constellations

More than half of today's constellations come from Greek mythology. Others were recorded more recently by astronomers and explorers between the 1500s and 1700s. Over the years, the official constellations have changed. Some have been split into smaller parts, others have been renamed, and a few have been removed altogether.

Stories of the stars

Greek astronomer Ptolemy listed 48 of the 88 recognized constellations. These were mostly based on popular characters from Greek or Roman mythology, such as this Auriga constellation that represents the King of Athens. Each constellation started as a shape in the sky, and soon a story unfolded.

Brightest star

While each constellation has a brightest star, the brightness can vary depending on the size of the star and how far away it is. A star's brightness is measured using a scale called magnitude. Brighter stars have lower magnitudes.

Sirius is the brightest star in the night sky with a magnitude of -1.46.

Area of a constellation

A constellation's shape is usually defined by joining some of its brightest stars, but its area extends beyond that. All stars within the boundary, including galaxies, nebulae, and other celestial objects, are considered to be "in" the constellation.

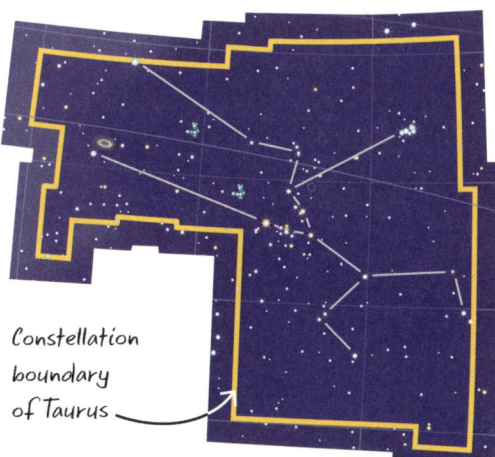

Constellation boundary of Taurus

Sombrero Galaxy

Deep-sky objects

Anything other than a single star or a planet in the sky is called a deep-sky object (DSO). This includes star clusters, nebulae, and galaxies. While each constellation is home to some DSOs, the ones closer to the Milky Way are the most spectacular.

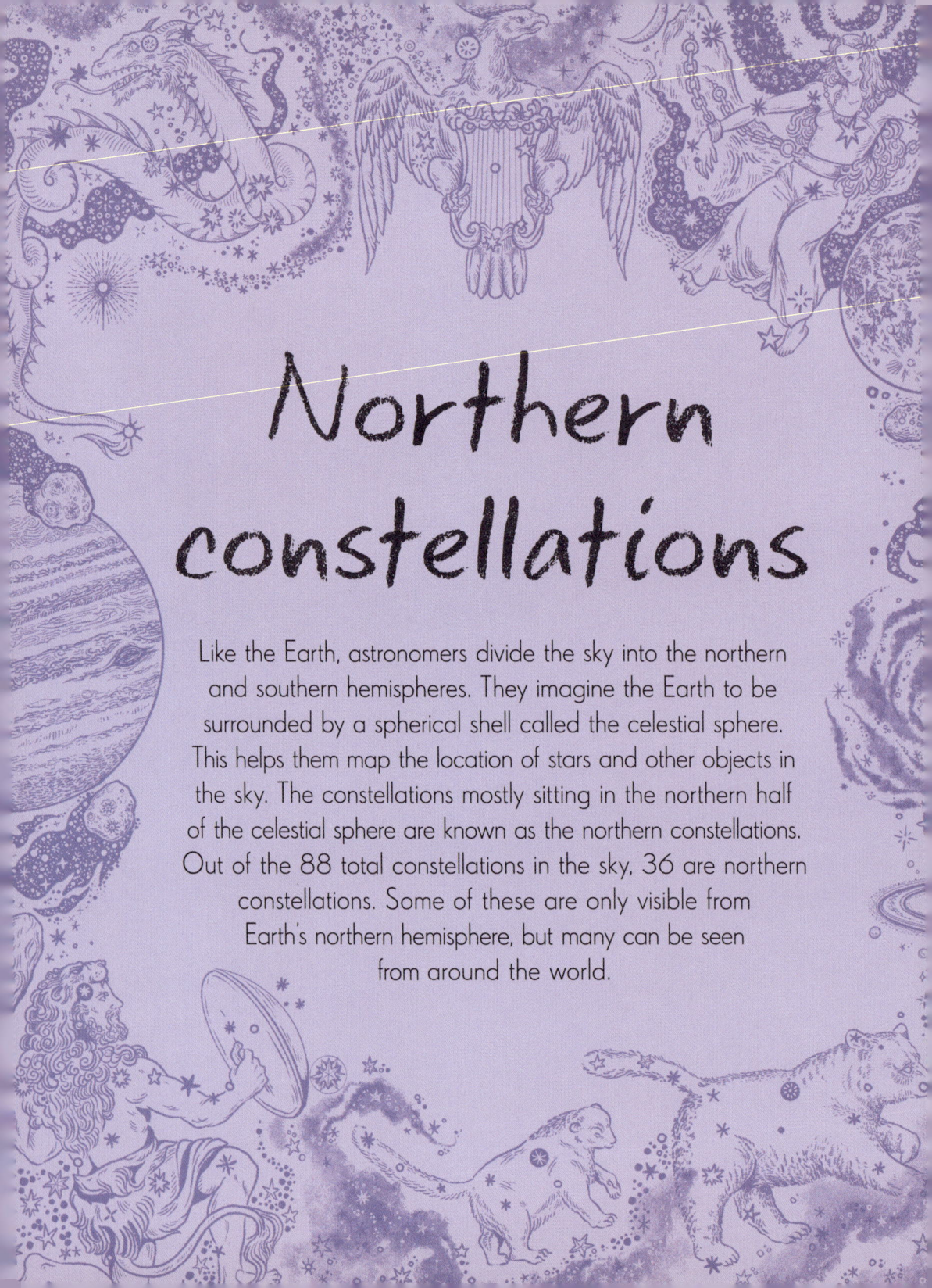

Northern constellations

Like the Earth, astronomers divide the sky into the northern and southern hemispheres. They imagine the Earth to be surrounded by a spherical shell called the celestial sphere. This helps them map the location of stars and other objects in the sky. The constellations mostly sitting in the northern half of the celestial sphere are known as the northern constellations. Out of the 88 total constellations in the sky, 36 are northern constellations. Some of these are only visible from Earth's northern hemisphere, but many can be seen from around the world.

Orion

The stars of Orion (oh-RAI-un) can be joined to form the shape of a hunter. It can be easily identified by looking for the three bright stars that make up Orion's belt. Just below it lies the Orion Nebula, a glowing cloud of dust and gas where new stars are constantly being born. Orion appears most clearly between November and January.

In Greek mythology, Orion is often shown holding a club in one hand and a lion's head in the other.

This star mostly appears to flicker in the night sky, a possible sign it's nearing the end of its life.

Betelgeuse

Orion's belt

Orion Nebula

Rigel

Andromeda

Look for the princess Andromeda (an-DROH-me-da) in the northern skies between August and February, and in the southern skies between October and December. This constellation contains the brilliant Andromeda Galaxy, one of the most distant objects you can see with the naked eye.

In Greek mythology, Princess Andromeda was rescued from a sea monster by Perseus. His constellation lies close to hers.

Andromeda Galaxy

This star marks the head of Princess Andromeda.

Alpheratz

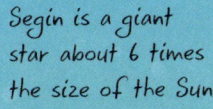
Segin is a giant star about 6 times the size of the Sun.

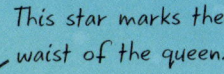
This star marks the waist of the queen.

Schedar

The constellation is often pictured as the queen sitting on a throne and admiring herself in a mirror.

Cassiopeia

Next to Andromeda sits her mother, Queen Cassiopeia (cass-ee-oh-PEE-uh). This constellation is easy to spot because its brightest stars form a W or M shape, depending on where you look from. Cassiopeia can be seen from the northern hemisphere all year round.

Perseus

In Greek mythology, Perseus was a hero who slayed the snake-haired monster, Medusa.

Perseus (PER-see-us) is home to one of the best meteor showers of the year, called the Perseids. The constellation's second-brightest star, Algol, contains two stars that orbit each other. One of them is dimmer and bigger, which makes the star that we see vary in brightness. Perseus can be best viewed in December in the northern skies.

It is one of the brightest stars in the night sky.

Mirfak

Algol's flickering light is often linked to Medusa's winking eye.

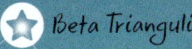 Beta Trianguli

Small, triangular shape makes it easy to spot

This star marks the head of the triangle and is called Caput Trianguli.

Triangulum

One of the smallest constellations in the night sky, Triangulum (try-ang-yuh-lum) gets its name from the triangular shape its bright stars make. It lies between Andromeda and Perseus and is best seen in December. Some early astronomers thought this constellation was part of the Plough, the star pattern in Ursa Major.

The ancient Greeks thought Triangulum looked like the Greek capital letter delta.

This is the sixth-brightest star in the night sky.

Capella

The star Elnath lies on the border of Auriga and Taurus.

Auriga is depicted as the King of Athens holding three goats.

Auriga

One of the largest constellations, Auriga (aw-RAI-guh), the charioteer, is most visible in February. It is surrounded by Taurus, Gemini, and Lynx. Capella, the brightest star in Auriga, is particularly exciting. When watched closely from the northern hemisphere in autumn, it flashes colours of red, green, and blue.

Camelopardalis

Camelopardalis (ca-mel-oh-PAR-duh-liss) was defined by Dutch astronomer Petrus Plancius in 1613. This constellation can be seen throughout the year from the northern hemisphere, but the best time to view it is in February. The long neck of Camelopardalis is believed to stretch around the north celestial pole.

Its brightest stars almost make a U shape.

Beta Camelopardalis

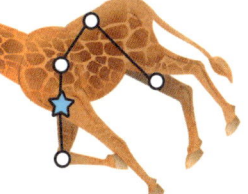

Camelopardalis was thought to represent an animal with the long neck of a camel and the spots of a leopard.

Canis Minor

Canis Minor (CAY-neez MAI-ner) is a small constellation made up of two shiny stars. It is sometimes considered as the smaller of Orion's two hunting dogs. Located close to Orion and Canis Major, this northern constellation appears most clearly in February. Its brightest star, Procyon, is part of a star pattern called the Winter Triangle.

The hunting dogs, Canis Minor and Canis Major, are thought to chase the Orion constellation.

This star, called Gomeisa, represents the dog's neck.

Procyon

Praecipua

This star is only visible on dark nights.

Leo Minor

A compact and dim constellation, Leo Minor (LEE-oh MAI-ner) is difficult to find in the night sky as it has no bright stars. The best time to spot it is in April from both the northern and southern skies. Polish astronomer Johannes Hevelius formed Leo Minor in 1687 from the three stars between Ursa Major and Leo.

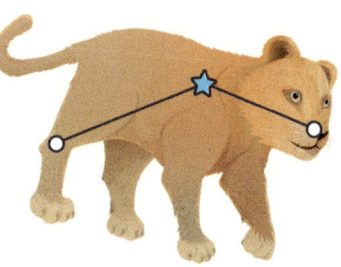

This constellation is also called the "little lion" because it represents the cub of the larger Leo, the lion.

This star marks the nose of the animal.

Tip of the Lynx's tail

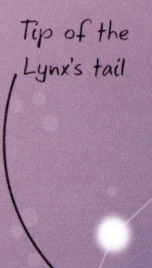
Alpha Lyncis

Lynx

Lynx (LINKS) hides in a dark stretch of sky between the brighter Gemini and Ursa Major. A clear view of this animal constellation, depicting a lynx, is possible from January to May.

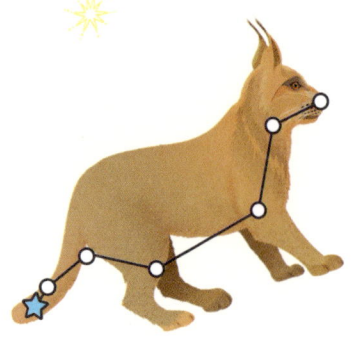

According to Hevelius, one would need the sharp eyes of a lynx to see this dim constellation.

Monoceros

High in the night sky, Monoceros (mo-NO-se-ros), the unicorn, gallops among the stars. This faint constellation can be seen from most parts of the world in February. It is easy to find because it sits within a triangle formed by three bright stars — Sirius in Canis Major, Procyon in Canis Minor, and Betelgeuse in Orion.

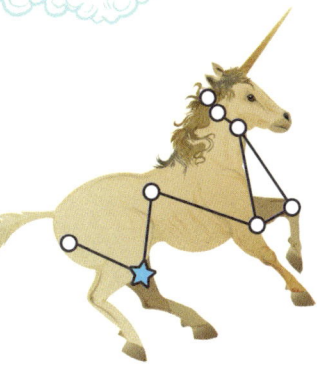

Monoceros looks as if it is running to the west, towards Orion.

This line of three stars stretches across the neck of the unicorn.

Alpha Monocerotis

Boötes

Pictured as a man guiding a bear, Boötes (bo-OH-teez) is named after the Greek word for "herdsman". The best time to see this large constellation is in April and May. Its brightest star, Arcturus, is known to release about 100 times more light than the Sun. The Egyptians thought of Boötes as a hippopotamus.

Boötes is often depicted with a staff in one hand and a sickle in the other.

Boötes contains an almost diamond-shaped pattern of stars called the Kite.

Arcturus

It is also the brightest star in the northern celestial hemisphere.

Alioth

The handle of the ladle-shaped Plough is used to locate Boötes.

This marks the hindleg of the bear.

Ursa Major

Ursa Major (ER-suh MAY-jur), the great bear, is the third-largest constellation and one of the most recognizable ones. This is mostly due to the well-known star pattern it contains called the Plough or Big Dipper. Ursa Major is visible all year round from the northern hemisphere. Astronomers often use it to find many other constellations in the night sky.

Ursa Major is associated with a Greek story about a woman who was turned into a bear.

Canes Venatici

Identified by Johannes Hevelius in 1687, Canes Venatici (CAY-neez ve-NA-tis-ai) is made up of two glimmering stars. It sits between Ursa Major and Boötes and appears most clearly in May. This constellation was considered part of Ursa Major until Hevelius separated the stars. Canes Venatici is also home to a popular spiral galaxy called the Whirlpool Galaxy.

Whirlpool Galaxy

This star marks the head of one of the hunting dogs.

Cor Caroli

The constellation is often imagined as a pair of hunting dogs held on a leash by Boötes.

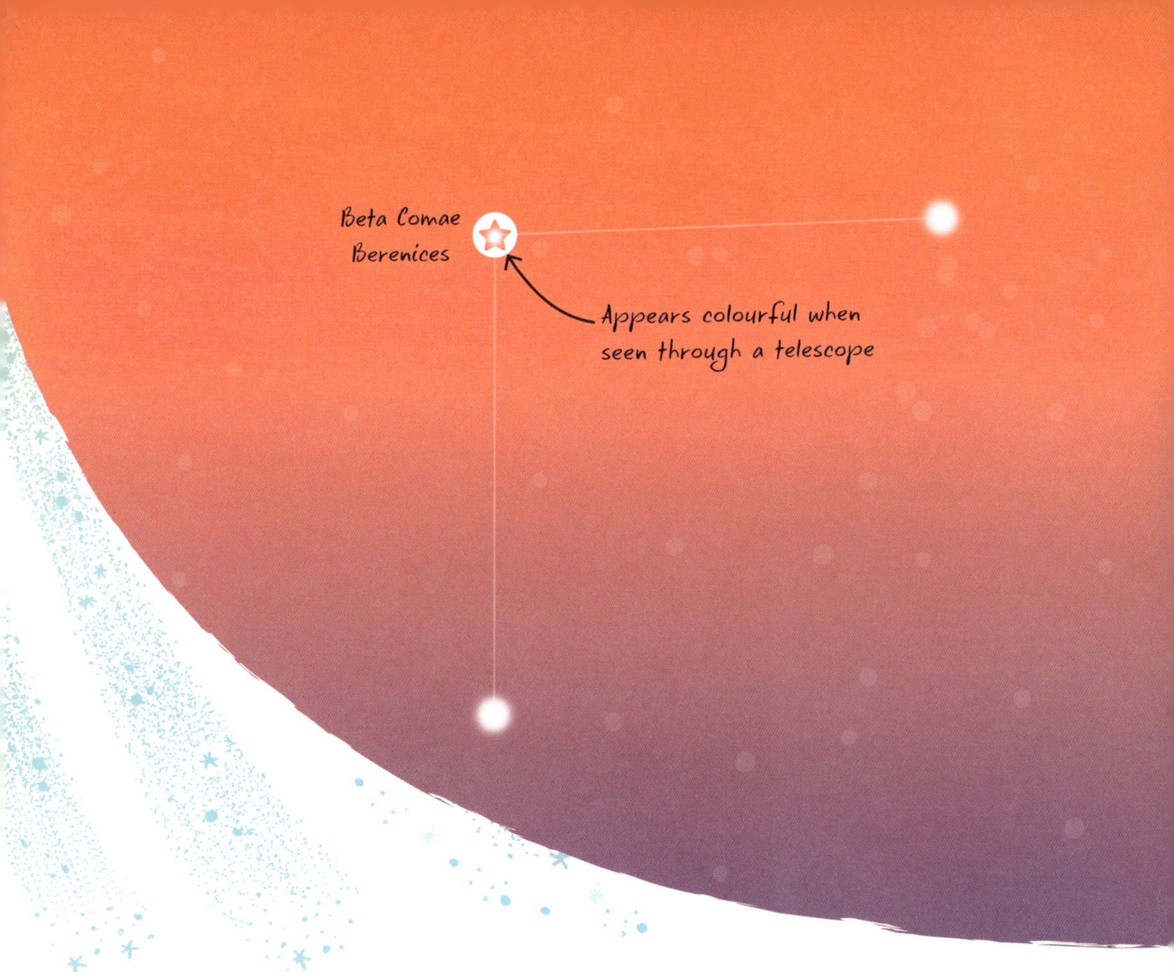

Beta Comae Berenices

Appears colourful when seen through a telescope

Coma Berenices

Visible from both hemispheres, Coma Berenices (COH-ma be-re-NAI-seez) is one of the smallest northern constellations. It is nestled inside a starry ring created by Leo, Virgo, Boötes, Canes Venatici, and Ursa Major. Although faint in appearance, Coma Berenices is most visible in May. It was once part of Leo but now belongs to the 88 official constellations.

The constellation depicts the locks of Queen Berenice II of Egypt.

Corona Borealis

Corona Borealis (cuh-ROH-na bo-ree-AL-iss) is a small, horseshoe-shaped constellation that lies between Hercules and Boötes. Though easy to find, its glowing arc stands out most clearly in June in both northern and southern skies. According to Greek mythology, Corona Borealis represents the crown worn by Princess Ariadne on her wedding day.

In a Greek myth, Ariadne's husband - the god Dionysus - threw her crown into the sky, turning its jewels into stars forever.

Ancient Arab astronomers saw this constellation as a bowl.

Alphecca

Unukalhai

Serpens Caput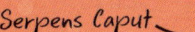

Serpens Cauda has no bright stars.

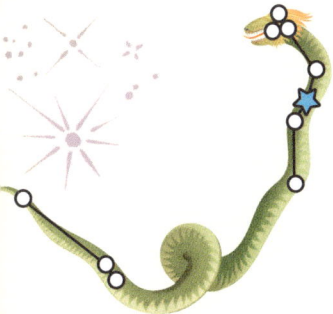

Serpens is named after a mythical snake slain by Ophiuchus, which then came back to life.

Serpens

Serpens (SER-punz) is a unique constellation as it has two parts — Serpens Caput, the head, and Serpens Cauda, the tail. Though imagined as one serpent, the parts are actually separated by the constellation Ophiuchus. This cosmic snake is best seen slithering across the northern and southern skies in July and August.

Hercules

The fifth-largest constellation in the sky, Hercules (HER-kyuh-leez) honours the Roman mythological hero of the same name. It rests besides Vega, the brightest star in the constellation Lyra. This celestial hero can be best seen in July, high in the northern skies.

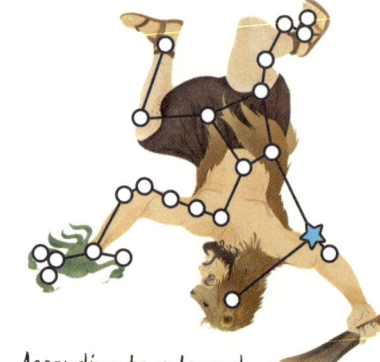

According to a legend, Hercules killed a Greek dragon, which is represented by the constellation Draco.

← Hercules's right foot

It contains a four-sided pattern called the Keystone.

 Kornephoros

This star, called Thuban, was thought to be the pole star 4,000 years ago.

Head of the dragon

Elatnin

Draco

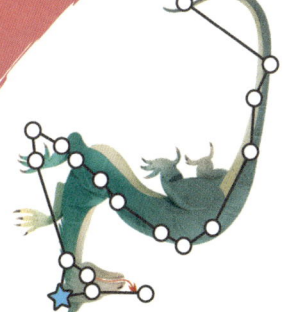

Draco is named after Ladon, the mythical Greek dragon who guarded the garden of golden apples.

Coiled around the North Star, Draco (DRAY-co) sits near the northern celestial pole. This means that if you are looking at it in the northern skies, it never sets. Draco is a large constellation but does not contain many bright stars. In Arabic astronomy, Draco is depicted as a herd of camels.

Polaris

For centuries, sailors have been using this star to find their way north.

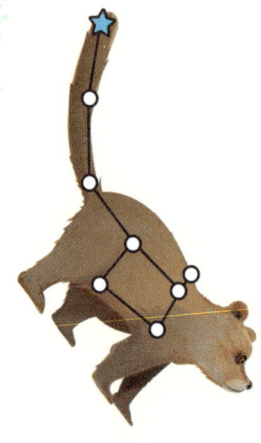

In Greek mythology, Zeus changed his son Arcas into a little bear and placed him in the sky. His mother, Ursa Major, is nearby.

Kochab and Phekad appear to circle around the North Star, so are known as the "Guardians of the Pole".

Kochab

Phekad

Ursa Minor

Ursa Minor (ER-suh MAI-ner) is visible in the northern skies all year round. It is also called the Little Dipper because its seven brightest stars form a smaller version of the Big Dipper. Its brightest star, Polaris or the North Star, sits roughly above the Earth's North Pole.

Aquila

The constellation Aquila (AK-will-uh), the eagle, soars near the centre of the Milky Way. So, it is surrounded by star clusters and swirling clouds of dust and gas called nebulae. Aquila is easy to find in the night sky because its brightest star, Altair, is part of the Summer Triangle. Look out for Aquila on August evenings.

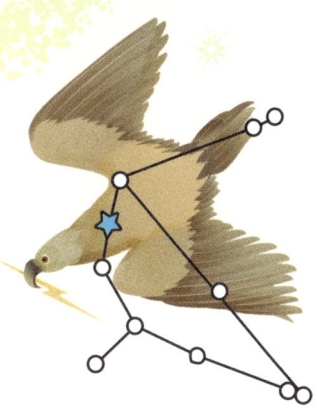

Aquila is known as "Maliyan", meaning "wedge-tailed eagle", in some First Australian traditions.

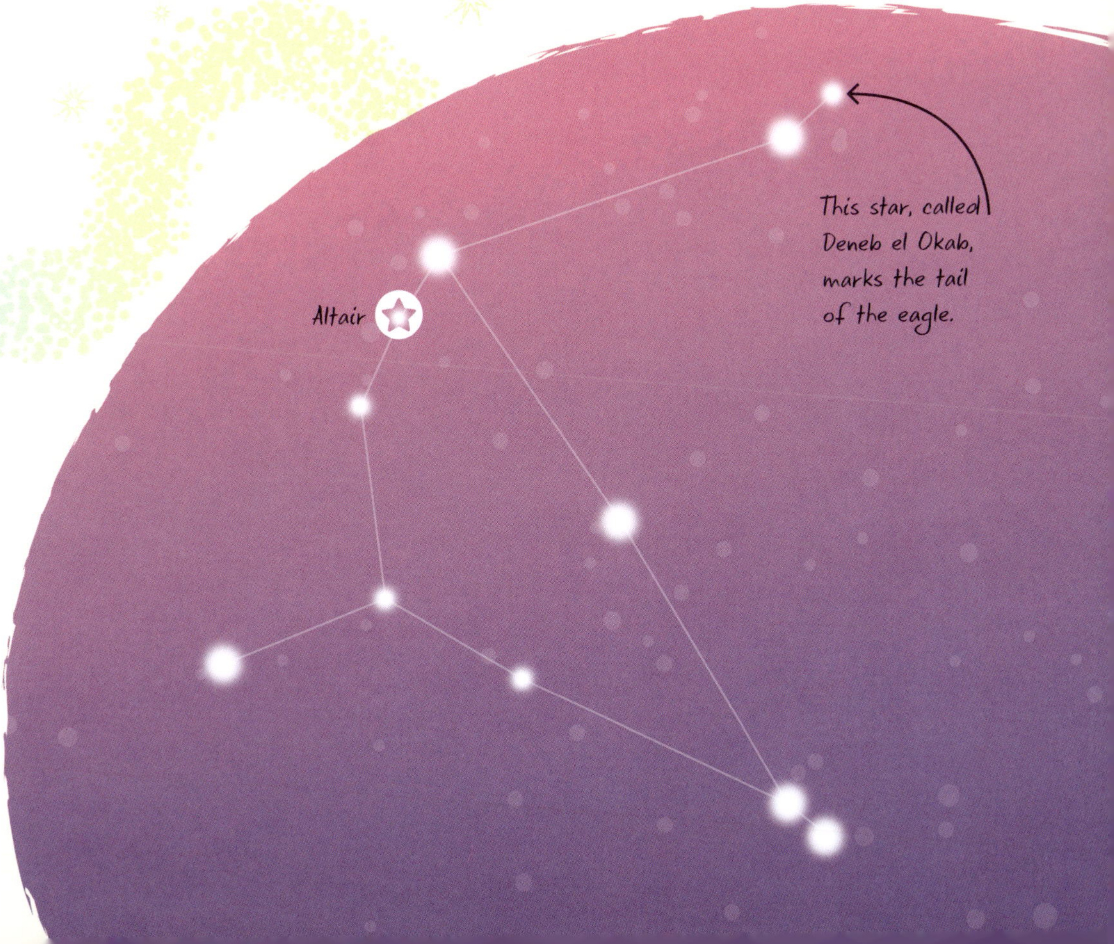

Altair

This star, called Deneb el Okab, marks the tail of the eagle.

Cepheus

Located near the northern celestial pole, Cepheus (SEE-fee-us) is visible from most of the northern hemisphere. This constellation can be clearly seen between September and November. It is home to one of the largest known black holes, which has a mass of about 40 billion times greater than that of the Sun. The mass of an object in space refers to the amount of material it contains.

In Greek mythology, Cepheus was the husband of Queen Cassiopeia and father of Andromeda.

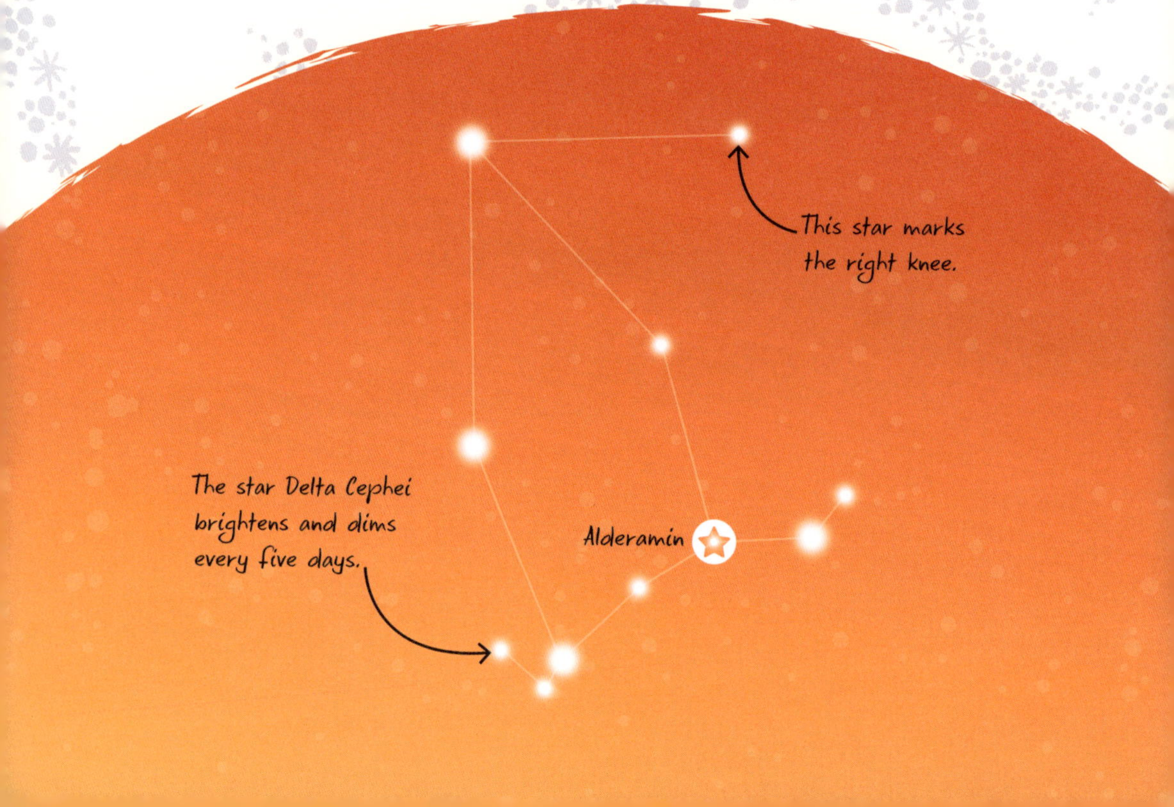

This star marks the right knee.

The star Delta Cephei brightens and dims every five days.

Alderamin

Shining at the swan's graceful end is Deneb, which means "tail" in Arabic.

Deneb

This star, called Albireo, marks the head of the swan or the foot of the cross.

In Chinese astronomy, Cygnus is located in the northern region of the sky known as the Black Tortoise of the North.

Cygnus

Cygnus (SIG-ness) stretches across the night sky like a swan in flight. It can be spotted easily due to the bright stars at its centre that form a cross. This cross is sometimes known as the Northern Cross. Visible from both hemispheres, the best time to view Cygnus is around September.

Rotanev

The diamond-shaped pattern is known as Job's Coffin.

Delphinus is depicted as a dolphin leaping out of the night sky.

Delphinus

With its curved shape and playful sparkle, Delphinus (del-FINE-us) is the starry dolphin of the night sky. The small, faint constellation swims between Pegasus and Aquila. It can be seen worldwide in September. The best way to spot Delphinus is by locating the Summer Triangle first, then going east (right) from Altair.

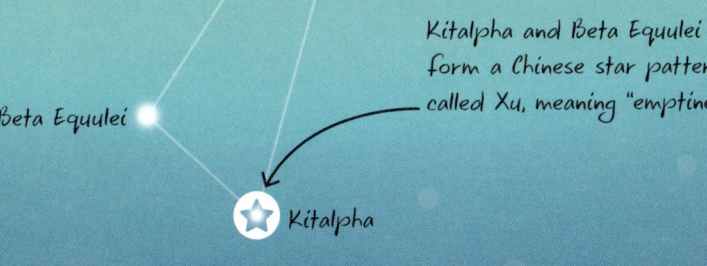

Beta Equulei

Kitalpha and Beta Equulei form a Chinese star pattern called Xu, meaning "emptiness".

Kitalpha

Equuleus

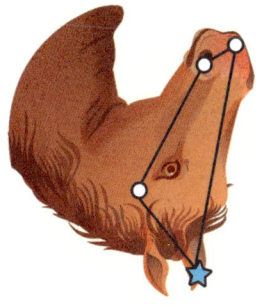

One Greek myth says Equuleus's foal-shaped head resembled that of the son of Pegasus, the winged horse.

Equuleus (ek-WOO-lee-us) is the second-smallest constellation in the dark sky. With only a few bright stars, it's a tricky one to spot. However, you can find it by looking for the Summer Triangle. Equuleus is visible from all around the world between August and November. Often imagined as the head of a foal, it is also called the "little horse".

Asterisms

Any star pattern in the sky that isn't one of the 88 official constellations is called an asterism. Some are made of stars from one constellation, while others include stars from different constellations. Well-known asterisms, such as the Summer Triangle and the Plough, help stargazers navigate the sky. If you spot patterns in the stars, you can make your own asterism too.

The Summer Triangle
This large pattern is made up of three stars from three constellations — Vega in Lyra, Altair in Aquila, and Deneb in Cygnus. Appearing directly overhead during summer in the northern hemisphere, it is used to locate many constellations.

The Plough
Also known as the Big Dipper, the Plough is an asterism in Ursa Major. This ladle-shaped asterism is sometimes imagined as a saucepan. The Plough can be used to find the North Star.

The Winter Hexagon

Trailing across the dark sky, the Winter Hexagon is formed by six stars from six winter constellations. This large northern asterism looks almost like a big circle, so is also called the Winter Circle. Once you know its stars, you can identify all six constellations.

The Southern Cross

This southern asterism sits in the Crux. For thousands of years, it has been used by sailors to locate the south celestial pole. The Southern Cross is also featured on the flags of many southern countries.

The Teapot

An asterism within Sagittarius, the Teapot sits near the centre of the Milky Way. The "steam" rising from its spout is actually the galaxy's disc. Just above it, you'll also find the Teaspoon, another asterism in Sagittarius.

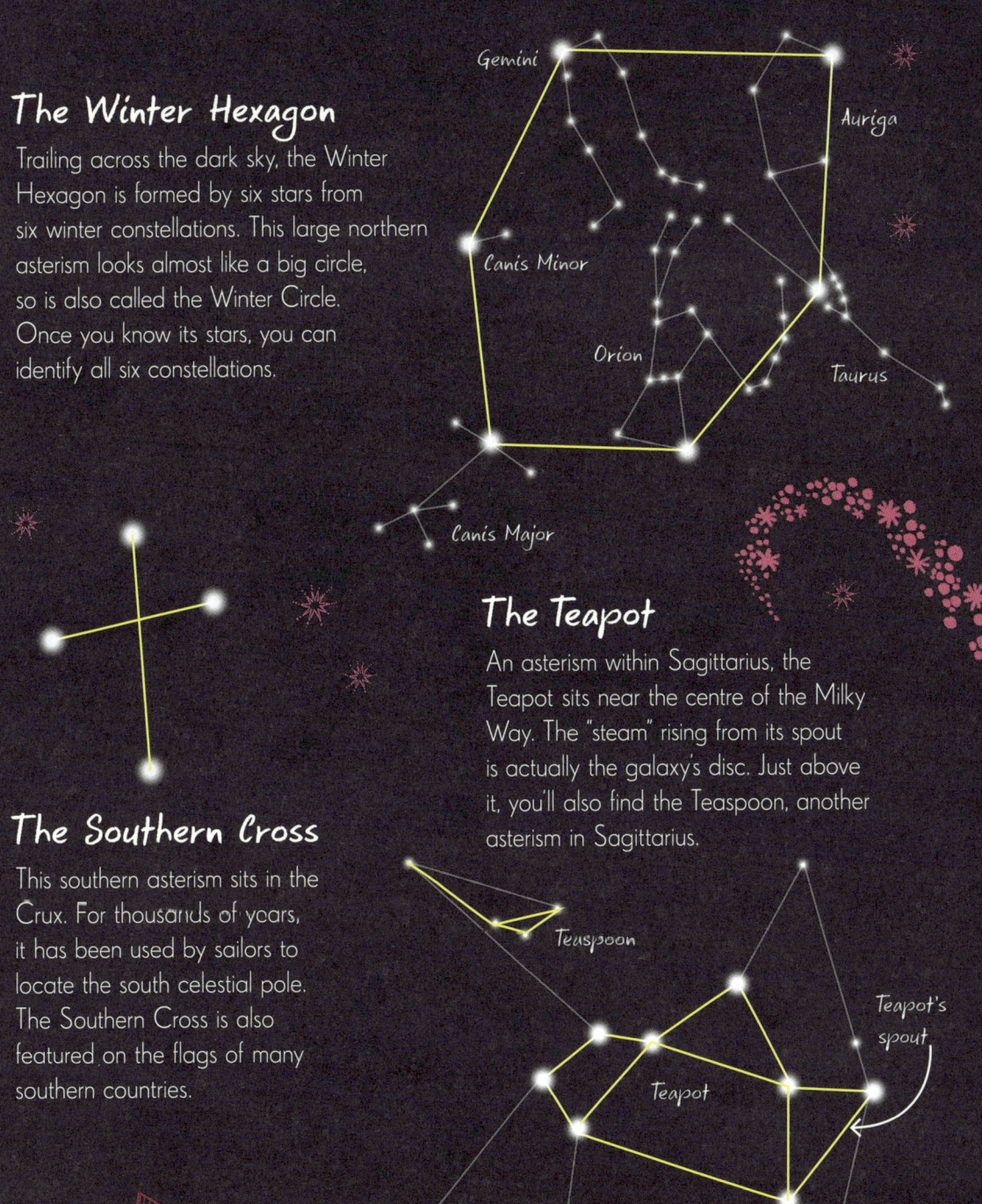

Lacerta

True to its name, Lacerta (luh-SER-tuh) scrambles across the sky like a lizard. Made up of faint stars, it's mostly noticeable in October. Lacerta lies on the edge of the Milky Way, surrounded by the brighter constellations Cassiopeia and Cygnus.

Lacerta was initially called Stellio, after a species of medium-sized lizard.

Alpha Lacertae

This star sits in the tail of the lizard.

Lyra

Lyra (LIE-rah), the harp, is an ancient constellation, first written by the astronomer Ptolemy in the 2nd century. While it can be seen for most of the year in the northern skies, the constellation is best visible in August. Every April, the Lyrid meteor shower appears to radiate from Lyra, lighting up the night sky.

This constellation is often thought to be the stringed instrument of the mythical Greek musician Orpheus.

This is the fifth-brightest star in the night sky.

Vega

Arab astronomers thought of Lyra as a soaring eagle.

51

Pegasus

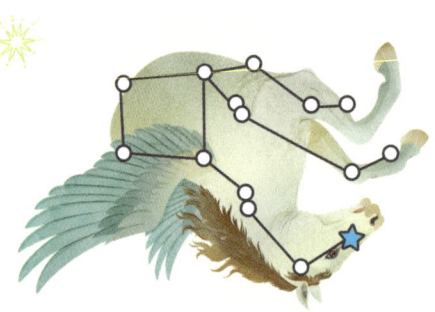

The ancient people of Mesopotamia knew Pegasus as a horse called Nimrod.

Pegasus (PEH-guh-sus), the winged horse, is one of the biggest constellations in the night sky. It is best viewed in October and can be found using The Great Square of Pegasus. This square star pattern is formed by three bright stars from Pegasus — Scheat, Markab, and Algenib — along with Alpheratz, a star shared between Pegasus and Andromeda.

This star depicts the head of Andromeda.

Alpheratz

Scheat

Algenib

Markab

Enif

52

In Greek mythology, Sagitta is often linked to the arrow Hercules shot to kill Zeus's eagle.

Delta Sagittae is a binary star system.

Gamma Sagittae

This star and the one above it mark the back of the arrow.

Sagitta

The third-smallest constellation, Sagitta (sa-GIT-uh) gets its name from the Latin word for "arrow". This faint constellation is identified by the arrow-like arrangement of its bright stars, and can be best seen piercing through the sky in September. Sagitta is located in the Milky Way, bordered by Vulpecula and Cygnus to the north and Aquila to the south.

This star marks the hindleg of the fox.

Anser

Dumbbell Nebula

This constellation was originally called Vulpecula et Anser, meaning "the little fox and the goose".

Vulpecula

The best time to look for Vulpecula (vul-PECK-yuh-luh), the little fox, is during summer in the northern hemisphere. This dim constellation is easy to spot due to its position within the well-known Summer Triangle. It is home to the Dumbbell Nebula, which looks like a round patch as big as a quarter of a full Moon.

Southern constellations

The constellations that lie mostly below the celestial equator and within the southern celestial hemisphere are called southern constellations. There are 52 southern constellations, of which 15 lie on the celestial equator. Many of the southern constellations can still be seen from the northern hemisphere, except those near the south celestial pole. The best view of the centre of the Milky Way is from the southern hemisphere. This is why the southern skies offer some of the most spectacular starry sights.

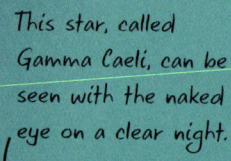

This star, called Gamma Caeli, can be seen with the naked eye on a clear night.

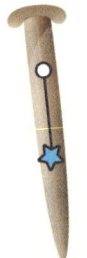

Caelum was first named Caelum Sculptorium, meaning "engraver's chisel" and later shortened to Caelum, which means "chisel".

Alpha Caeli

Caelum

Caelum (SEE-lum) was identified by French astronomer Nicolas Louis de Lacaille in the 1750s. This faint constellation of the southern skies has very few bright stars, and is best viewed from December to January. Caelum is the eighth-smallest constellation in the night sky.

Cetus

Cetus (SEE-tus) was named after a mythical whale-like sea monster. It sits in a part of the sky known as the "heavenly waters". This region contains many other constellations associated with water – including Eridanus, the river, Aquarius, the water bearer, and Pisces, the fish. Spot Cetus floating in the heavenly waters on December evenings.

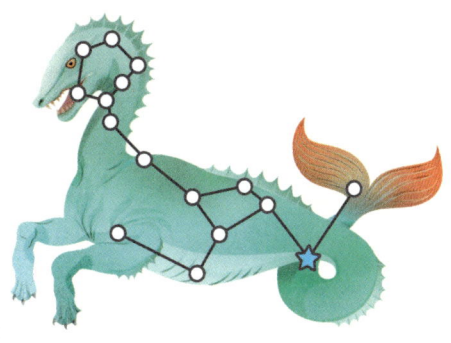

The people from the ancient city of Babylon (in modern-day Iraq) named it Tiamat, after their sea goddess.

The star Mira brightens and dims as it grows and shrinks every 11 months.

This star makes the tail of the sea monster.

Diphda

↙ This star sits
at the tail
of the hare.

Arneb

← It is a dying star,
expected to explode
within a million years.

Lepus

Resting under the feet of Orion, Lepus (LEEP-us) appears to be chased across the night sky by the dog constellations — Canis Major and Canis Minor. This dim, medium-sized constellation can be seen from most parts of the world in January.

Lepus, the hare, is usually drawn with two long ears.

Columba

Tucked between Canis Major and Lepus, Columba (cuh-LUM-buh), the dove, can be best spotted in January. Its stars were once considered to be part of Canis Major until the 1500s. But Dutch astronomer Petrus Plancius made it into a separate constellation, using leftover stars between Canis Major and Lepus that were not part of any other constellation.

This star appears blue-white in colour when seen through a telescope.

Phact

Eta Columbae marks the head of the dove.

Columba was once called Columba Noachi, meaning "Noah's Dove", after the dove in the story of Noah's Ark.

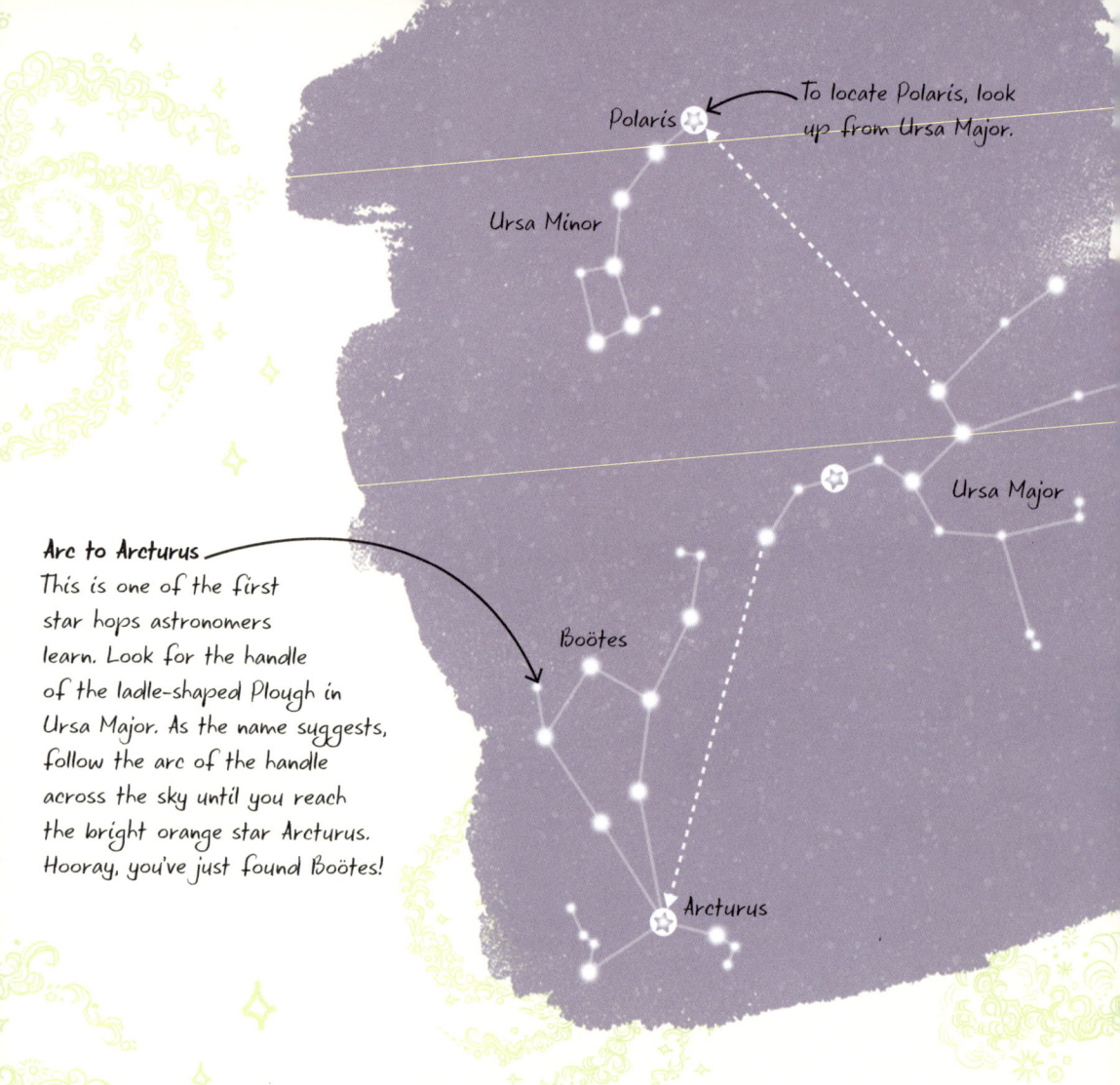

To locate Polaris, look up from Ursa Major.

Polaris

Ursa Minor

Ursa Major

Arc to Arcturus
This is one of the first star hops astronomers learn. Look for the handle of the ladle-shaped Plough in Ursa Major. As the name suggests, follow the arc of the handle across the sky until you reach the bright orange star Arcturus. Hooray, you've just found Boötes!

Boötes

Arcturus

Star hopping

Some constellations are easier to spot than others. This is because of their recognizable patterns or especially bright stars. Stargazers often use these constellations as guides to find other constellations and asterisms in the sky. This is called star hopping. Constellations like Ursa Major and Crux are great for this. They act like starry beacons, pointing to other wonders in the night sky.

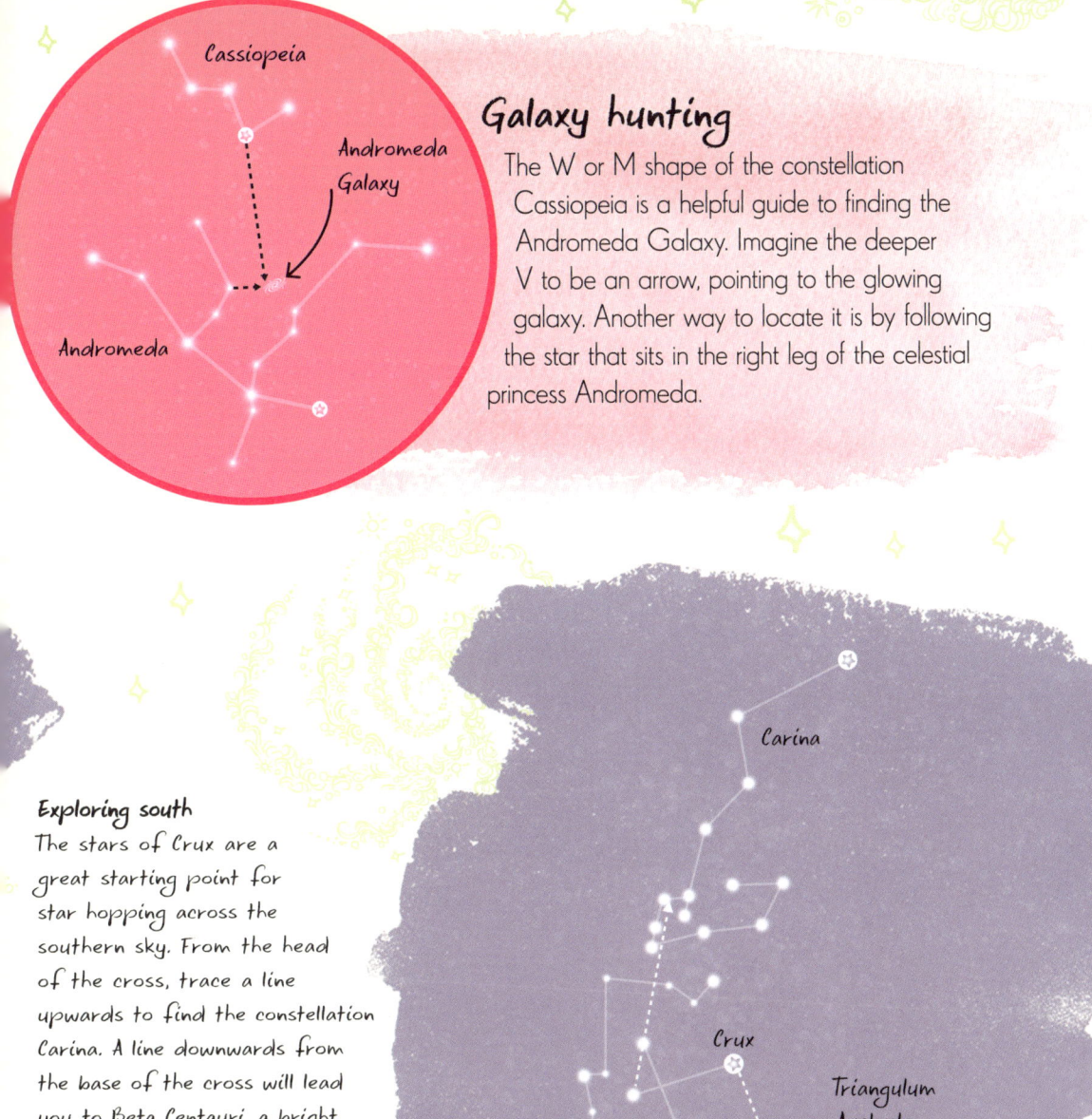

Galaxy hunting

The W or M shape of the constellation Cassiopeia is a helpful guide to finding the Andromeda Galaxy. Imagine the deeper V to be an arrow, pointing to the glowing galaxy. Another way to locate it is by following the star that sits in the right leg of the celestial princess Andromeda.

Exploring south

The stars of Crux are a great starting point for star hopping across the southern sky. From the head of the cross, trace a line upwards to find the constellation Carina. A line downwards from the base of the cross will lead you to Beta Centauri, a bright star in Centaurus. A short hop from the nearby Alpha Centauri points to Triangulum Australe.

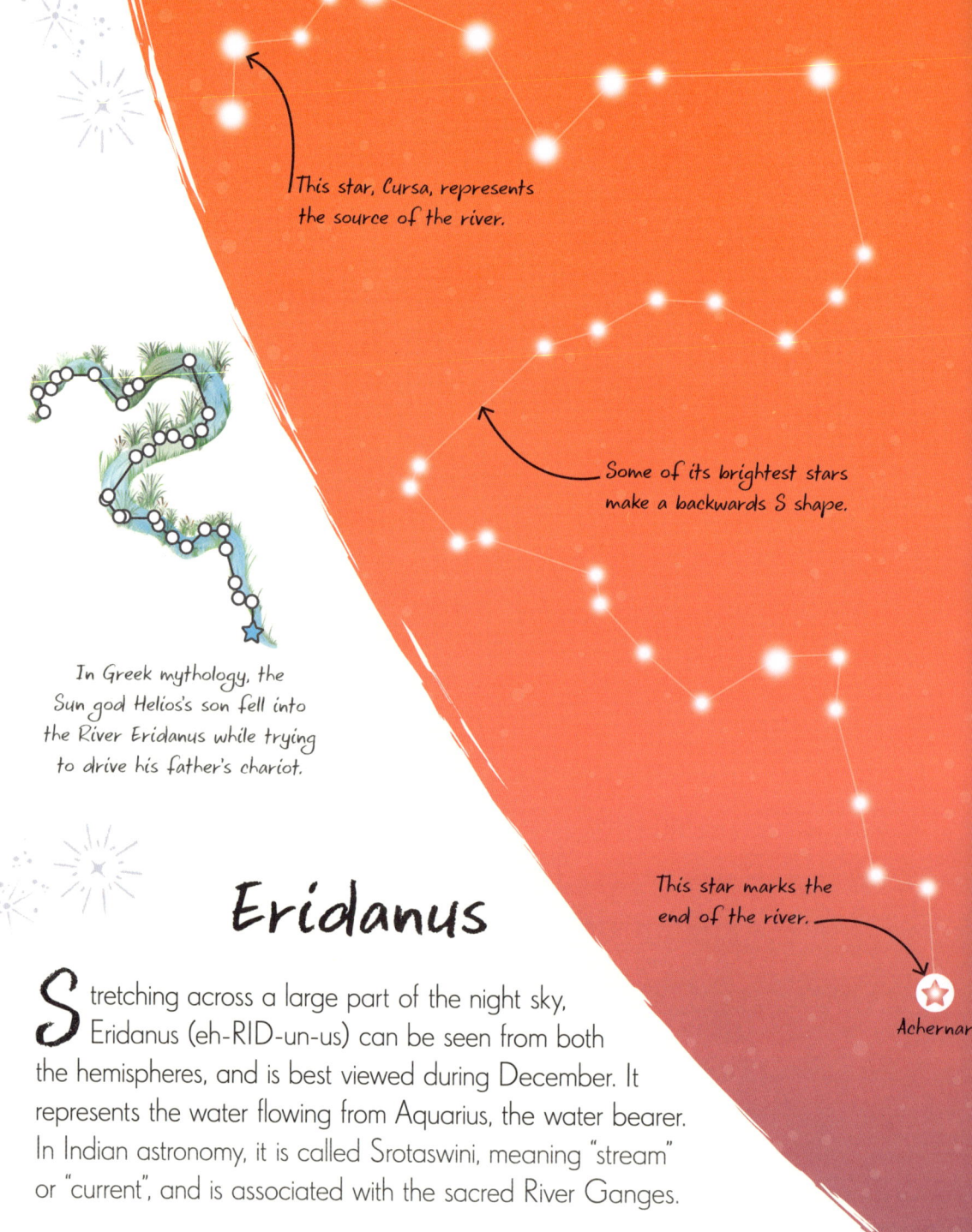

This star, Cursa, represents the source of the river.

Some of its brightest stars make a backwards S shape.

In Greek mythology, the Sun god Helios's son fell into the River Eridanus while trying to drive his father's chariot.

This star marks the end of the river.

Achernar

Eridanus

Stretching across a large part of the night sky, Eridanus (eh-RID-un-us) can be seen from both the hemispheres, and is best viewed during December. It represents the water flowing from Aquarius, the water bearer. In Indian astronomy, it is called Srotaswini, meaning "stream" or "current", and is associated with the sacred River Ganges.

The three bright stars seem to be linked to form a wide V shape.

It was originally called Fornax Chemica, meaning "the chemical furnace" in Latin.

Fornax

Fornax (FOR-naks), the furnace, is one of the many constellations introduced by Nicholas Louis de Lacaille in the 1700s. The heavenly furnace glows softly in the southern skies, appearing most clearly in December. It is home to a fascinating cluster that contains 58 galaxies.

Horologium

Horologium (hor-oh-LOH-jee-um), the clock, is a tiny constellation, faintly visible in the southern skies. It is home to a huge structure made up of about 5,000 groups of galaxies. On a clear December evening, the constellation can be easily identified by the line of three stars that sit on the clock's face.

It was earlier named Horologium Oscillatorium, after a pendulum clock used by astronomers for timekeeping.

Alpha Horologii — This star is imagined as the pendulum of the clock.

One of the lines of three stars

This star, named Alpha Hydri, sits at the head of the water snake.

Beta Hydri

Hydrus

Hydrus (HAI-drus) is a long and winding constellation that lies next to the two celestial birds — Tucana, the toucan, and Pavo, the peacock. This southern constellation slips quietly between stars, and is best seen in October and November.

Hydrus depicts a small male water snake, which is a less grand version of its larger cousin Hydra.

65

Alpha Doradus

This line stretches across the body of the fish.

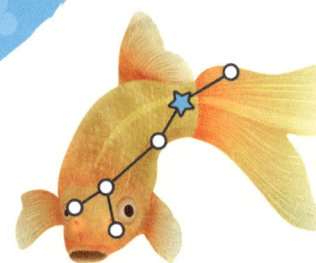
Although known as Dolphinfish, Dorado is often depicted as a goldfish or sometimes a swordfish.

Dorado

Dorado (doh-RAH-do) is a compact but significant constellation as it contains more than half of the Large Magellanic Cloud. This is a small galaxy that orbits the Milky Way and is known for its regions where new stars are born. Though faint, Dorado is best seen sparkling in the southern skies in January.

Mensa

A winter constellation, Mensa (MEN-suh) is the dimmest of the 88 modern constellations. It is so far down south that it's impossible to see from the northern hemisphere. Mensa is named after Table Mountain near Cape Town, South Africa. This is where Lacaille observed the southern skies when recording a group of new constellations.

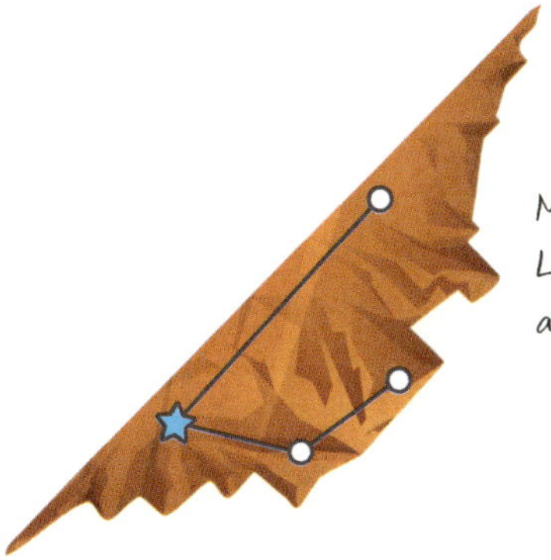

Mensa is the only constellation Lacaille did not name after an instrument.

This star, along with Alpha Mensae, lies at the base of the mountain.

Alpha Mensae

It is the faintest of all the bright stars in the night sky.

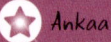 Ankaa

The star Zeta Phoenicis is a binary star that flickers in the sky.

The three stars arranged in a line make the bird's left wing.

Phoenix

Phoenix (FEE-nix) is a small, faint constellation in the southern skies, sometimes also visible from the southern edges of the northern hemisphere. The best time to look for it is on clear November evenings. Named after a mythical bird, it is one of the four southern bird constellations, along with Tucana, Pavo, and Grus.

The outline of stars in Phoenix looks like a bird in the sky. Chinese astronomers called it the "firebird".

Pictor

Pictor (PICK-ter) was originally named Equuleus Pictoris, which is the Latin word for "painter's easel". It was later changed to Pictor, but it was still commonly referred to as an easel. The best time to catch a glimpse of this constellation is in December. Its second-brightest star, Beta Pictoris, is surrounded by a disc of dust where planets are continuously forming.

Beta Pictoris

This star's temperature is about 7,500-10,000 K, while our Sun's is about 5,778 K.

Alpha Pictoris

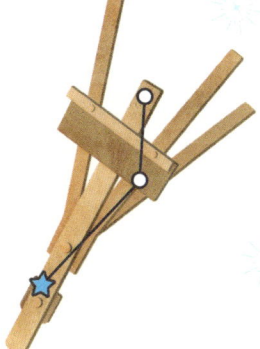

The constellation is still represented as an easel, though its name has been shortened to Pictor, meaning "painter".

Reticulum

Reticulum (re-TIK-yoo-lum) was first named Rhombus by German astronomer Isaac Habrecht II in the 1600s. Later, Nicolas Louis de Lacaille renamed it Reticulum, meaning "net". Most identifiable in January, the four brightest stars of this constellation form a rhombus or diamond-like shape.

A planet about the size of Jupiter orbits this star, Epsilon Reticuli.

Alpha Reticuli

The constellation depicts a tool called a grid or reticle, used in telescopes to work out the position of stars.

Alpha Sculptoris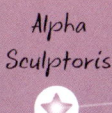

This star sits at the base of the sculpture.

Nicolas Louis de Lacaille first imagined this constellation as a sculptor's workshop, but its name has since been changed to "sculpture".

Sculptor

High in the southern sky, the stars of Sculptor (SCULP-ter) can be best seen from October to November. It is home to the South Galactic Pole, which lies to the south of the Milky Way. This area has no gas or dust, so it offers a clear view into the Universe beyond our galaxy, where many far-off galaxies can be seen.

71

Myths and legends

For thousands of years, people have looked at the stars and told stories about their shapes. The names of many modern constellations come from Greek mythology, but people worldwide have their own celestial stories. These tales often help us remember how different constellations are connected.

The hunter

Orion, the hunter, is linked to many Greek myths. One says he was the sea god Poseidon's son. In the sky, Orion is followed by his two dogs, Canis Major and Canis Minor, and together they chase Lepus the hare.

Ancient Sumerian astronomers saw Orion as the hero Gilgamesh, who was known to battle and overpower lions.

Seven sages

Ancient Indian astronomers knew the stars we now call the Plough, or Big Dipper, as the Saptarishi (sap-TA-ree-shee). These were seven wise men who were believed to be related to the gods and able to predict the future.

Fish hook

Early Hawaiian astronomers saw the body and tail of the constellation Scorpius as Manaiakalani (mah-NAH-ee-ah-kah-LAH-nee), the fish hook of the demigod Maui.

Maui's fish hook was thought to have pulled up islands from the ocean.

Great Celestial Emu

First Nations Australian astronomers identified this pattern of stars located in the Milky Way. The body of Emu is a cloud of darkness formed by dust. Its changing position in the sky helped people know when to collect emu eggs.

Starlit love

A Chinese myth tells of Vega and Altair, stars from Lyra and Aquila. The sky princess Vega fell in love with the cowherd Altair, but her father, the sky king, disapproved. He then placed them in the night sky as stars, separated by the Milky Way.

Stories also say that once a year magpies form a bridge across the Milky Way so the lovers can meet.

Antlia

Antlia (ANT-lee-uh) is a low-light constellation best viewed on clear April evenings. Three of its stars can be joined to make a triangle. It is home to the Antlia Cluster, a group of about 230 galaxies that can be seen using a large telescope. In Chinese astronomy, the stars of Antlia were thought to be part of two different constellations.

Antlia is named after an air pump, an 18th-century invention widely used in scientific experiments.

Alpha Antliae

This line marks one of the legs of Antlia.

Sirius

This is the brightest star in the night sky.

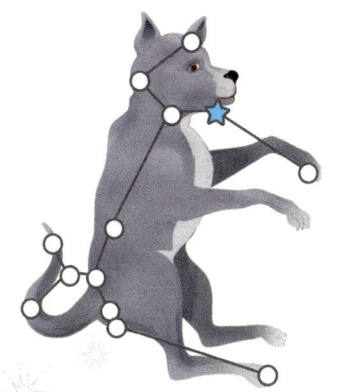

In Greek mythology, Canis Major was destined to catch anything it chased!

Canis Major

Canis Major (CAY-neez MAY-jer) was first introduced as a constellation by Ptolemy in the 2nd century. It is often imagined as the bigger one of Orion's hunting dogs. As the Earth rotates, it seems as if Canis Major is following Orion across the sky. Look for this dog constellation in February using its brightest star, Sirius, as your guide.

Eta Carinae alternates between brightening and dimming, like a shimmering light.

Canopus

Carina Nebula

The old constellation Argo Navis was depicted with large oars emerging near the keel.

Carina

Carina (cuh-REE-nuh) was once part of a larger constellation called Argo Navis, which represented a boat. Later, it was split into three parts, with Carina as the keel, or bottom part, of the ship. It contains the Carina Nebula, one of the largest clouds of dust in the sky. Carina appears to shine most clearly in March skies.

Chamaeleon

Chamaeleon (cuh-MI-lee-un) is one of the smallest constellations visible all year round from the southern hemisphere. This faint constellation is easy to find because it nestles between the Southern Cross and the southern celestial pole. When using the Southern Cross to find south, one may spot Chamaeleon along the path.

It was noted as Chamaeleon by Petrus Plancius in the 1500s, but in Australia it was referred to as the Frying Pan.

 Alpha Chamaeleontis

This star sits under the reptile's eye.

Labrum

Forms an almost square-shaped pattern

In Greek mythology, this constellation represented Apollo's drinking cup. He sent his bird, Corvus, to fetch water in it.

Crater

The word "crater" means a hole in the ground, but this constellation is named after the Greek word "krater", meaning a kind of cup. Best visible in April, Crater (CRAY-ter) has no bright stars. It sits next to Corvus, the crow.

Hydra

Slithering across the night sky, Hydra (HAI-druh) — the female water snake — is the biggest and longest of all 88 constellations. It is one of the two snake constellations — both Hydra and Hydrus date back to ancient times. Hydra can be mostly viewed in January and February from all over the world. Despite its huge size, the constellation has few bright stars.

According to Greek myth, Hydra was a nine-headed monster with one indestructible head.

Hydra covers more than a quarter of the celestial sphere.

Alphard

Head of the snake

Puppis

Puppis (PUP-iss) was once part of the ship constellation Argo Navis, which was later divided into three parts. Puppis is the largest of them. It particularly lights up the southern skies in February and peeks into the north near the equator. To find Puppis, locate Sirius, the brightest star in Canis Major. Puppis follows behind this greater dog constellation.

The ship's rear appears to sail along the Milky Way.

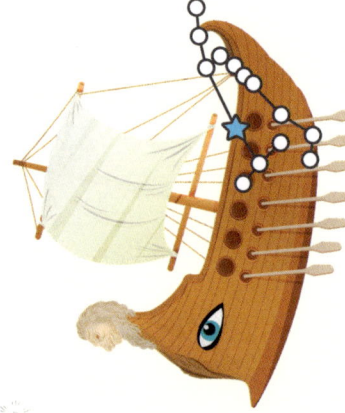

The name "poop deck" comes from the deck located at the rear (back) of the ship.

 Naos

To locate Pyxis, look for these three stars that appear in an almost straight line.

Alpha Pyxidis

Pyxis

A tiny constellation, Pyxis (PIX-iss) sits next to Puppis in the night sky. It can be seen in the southern skies between February and March. This constellation is home to the famous nova T Pyxidis. A nova occurs in a binary star system when one of the star partners suddenly brightens before gradually fading back to its original light.

The constellation was originally named Pyxis Nautica, meaning "mariner's compass", a tool that sailors use to find their way at sea.

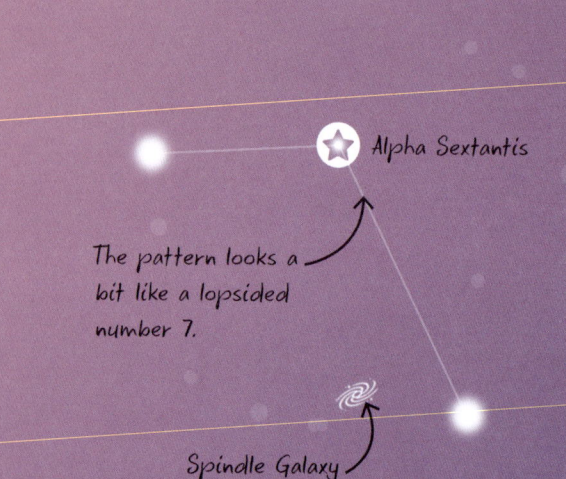

The pattern looks a bit like a lopsided number 7.

Alpha Sextantis

Spindle Galaxy

A sextant is a tool sailors use to find direction at sea by measuring the angle between a star and the horizon (where sky meets ground).

Sextans

Sextans (SEX-tunz) was identified in the 1600s by Johannes Hevelius. This dim constellation is most clearly visible on April evenings, twinkling in a faint patch of sky near the celestial equator. Sextans contains the Spindle Galaxy, which looks like a flat, round, thin disc.

Gamma Velorum

This star marks the top of the sail.

The stars of Vela form a pattern that resembles the flowing sails of a ship.

Vela

Vela (VEE-luh) represents the sail of the old ship constellation Argo Navis. It harbours a huge structure called the Vela Supercluster, which is a massive group of thousands of galaxies. Look for Vela's shining outline in the southern skies in March.

Volans

In the night sky, Volans (VOH-lanz) lies beside the constellation Carina and looks as if it's being chased by Dorado, the dolphinfish. This southern constellation is best viewed in February and can also be spotted from parts of the northern hemisphere near the equator.

Volans is often pictured as a fish leaping from the sea and gliding through the air.

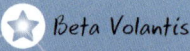 Beta Volantis

Its stars can be joined to make two triangles sitting next to each other.

Alpha Apodis

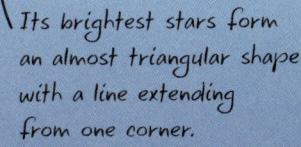

Its brightest stars form an almost triangular shape with a line extending from one corner.

The Bird of Paradise is native to New Guinea and the Maluku Islands.

Apus

Best seen in July, the small, dim Apus (APE-us) soars silently through the night sky. It lies near the south celestial pole, so its stars never set below the horizon. Originally named "Apis Indica", meaning "bird of paradise", it was later renamed after the Greek word "apous", meaning "without feet". This is because people once mistakenly believed the bird had no feet.

Alpha Arae spins so rapidly that it may soon cause particles to break away from its surface.

Beta Arae

Ara, the altar, was called "Al Mijmarah" by Arab astronomers, meaning "the incense lamp".

Ara

Ara (AR-uh) is one of the original 48 Greek constellations recorded by Ptolemy in the 2nd century. Located near the tail of the constellation Scorpius, it can be best spotted in June. Ancient astronomers in Australia saw Ara and nearby Pavo as a pair of fruit bats.

Centaurus

Centaurus (sen-TOR-us) is one of the largest constellations in the night sky. The best time to see Centaurus is in March, only from the southern hemisphere and the lower half of the northern hemisphere. Three of the closest stars to Earth — Alpha Centauri A, Alpha Centauri B, and Proxima Centauri — are all part of Centaurus.

It is linked to the Greek centaur Chiron. Centaurs were half-human, half-horse mythical creatures.

This star marks the right elbow of the centaur.

Omega Centauri is a bright star cluster made up of about 10 million stars.

Alpha Centauri

Circinus

Circinus (SER-sin-us) was introduced by Nicolas Louis de Lacaille in the mid-1700s. It sits in a faint patch of sky between Centaurus and Triangulum Australe. The best time to view Circinus is in June, by first locating the larger, brighter Centaurus nearby.

This constellation depicts a dividing compass, which is used to measure distances on maps.

Its three stars make a narrow, almost triangular shape.

Alpha Circini

Gienah

Marks the head of the crow

According to a legend, Corvus lied to the Greek god Apollo, so it was cast into the sky along with the cup Crater and the water snake Hydra.

Corvus

Named after the Latin word for "crow", Corvus (COR-vus) represents one of Apollo's sacred birds. Arab astronomers, however, saw a ship's sail in the stars of Corvus. This small, boxy constellation appears in the dark sky near Spica — Virgo's brightest star — and is best seen in May.

Crux

Although the smallest of the 88 modern constellations, Crux (CRUX) is one of the easiest to find in the southern skies. Since its bright stars point towards the south celestial pole, it has long helped explorers find their way. Crux also contains a colourful star cluster called the Jewel Box.

The four brightest stars of Crux are placed close to each other and form a distinct star pattern called the Southern Cross.

Through a telescope, the Jewel Box looks like a box of precious gems.

Acrux

This star sits in the head of the wolf.

Alpha Lupi

In a Greek myth, Lupus was offered as a sacrifice to the gods by the centaur Chiron.

Lupus

Lupus (LOOP-us) is one of the early constellations listed by Ptolemy. It is surrounded by the two larger and brighter neighbours — Centaurus and Scorpius. A good time to see Lupus, the wolf, is in July.

Left wing of the fly

Alpha Muscae

Its four brightest stars form a box-like shape in the sky.

Its northern partner, Musca Borealis, is now part of Aries.

Musca

Buzzing just below the Southern Cross lies the small constellation Musca (MUSS-kah). To find it, first locate Crux, then trace a line downwards from the cross. This tiny, starry fly is best seen in May. Musca was first called Musca Australis, the southern fly.

Norma

Astronomer Nicolas Louis de Lacaille named this constellation in the 1700s, along with other southern constellations. The stars of Norma (NOR-mah) are faint, but because it lies in the path of the Milky Way, it hosts a rich collection of galaxies. The best time to look for Norma is on June evenings.

Gamma-2 Normae

Its brightest star is so faint that it barely stands out from the nearby stars.

Norma is one of several constellations named after tools used for measuring and drawing.

Triangulum Australe

Triangulum Australe (try-ANG-yuh-lum aw-STRAY-leh) is one of the two triangle constellations. It gets its name from the triangle its three brightest stars make. It is located near the south celestial pole and is brighter than its northern partner with a similar name. The best time to view Triangulum Australe is in May, from the southern hemisphere.

It was earlier named Libella, meaning "the level", after a tool used to measure straight lines.

This star, Beta Trianguli, and Gamma Trianguli are similar in brightness.

Atria

Gamma Trianguli

Alphecca Meridiana

The constellation can be easily recognized by its horseshoe-shaped pattern.

Corona Australis

Like its northern twin Corona Borealis, Corona Australis (cuh-ROH-na aw-STRAL-iss) forms an arc of twinkling stars in the southern sky. This constellation is clearly visible in August, softly glowing in the skies of both hemispheres. Early Islamic astronomers saw this constellation as a tortoise.

Sitting near the archer Sagittarius, Corona Australis looks like the archer's crown.

Grus

Grus (GROOS) sits alongside the southern birds — Tucana, the toucan, and Phoenix, the firebird. The best time to marvel at this flying crane is in October from the southern hemisphere. However, it is also visible from the southern parts of the northern hemisphere, where it appears low in the sky.

Grus was once seen as the tail of the nearby Piscis Austrinus, the southern fish, but was separated in the 1700s.

Alnair

This star, called Beta Gruis or Tiaki, shines almost 2,500 times brighter than the Sun.

Indus

This constellation was introduced in the 1500s by Petrus Plancius. Indus (IN-dus) is thought to represent a traditional man wearing a ceremonial headdress and holding arrows in both hands. Indus appears most clearly in September in the southern skies.

This star marks the left elbow of the man.

Alpha Indi

The celestial man sits between three bird constellations – Tucana, Grus, and Pavo.

Microscopium

Microscopium (mai-cro-SCO-pee-um) is a small, faint constellation tucked between the brighter Piscis Austrinus and Sagittarius. It is most visible in the southern hemisphere but can also be seen from the lower half of the northern hemisphere.

Gamma Microscopii

Microscopium is one of the 18th-century constellations named after advanced scientific instruments.

Its stars form a nearly rectangular shape.

The constellation looks like a fish-shaped kite.

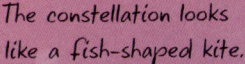
Fomalhaut

This star marks the mouth of the fish.

Piscis Austrinus

Known to Babylonian astronomers as the fish, Piscis Austrinus (pis-is aw-STRY-nus) was once part of the larger constellation Piscis Notius, meaning "great fish". Its brightest star, Fomalhaut, is nicknamed "the loneliest star" because it shines alone in a vast stretch of dark sky. Piscis Austrinus is best viewed in October.

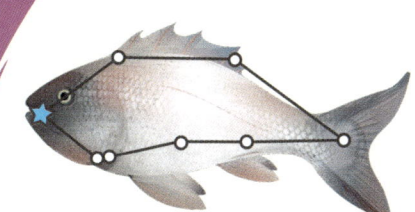

It depicts a fish with its mouth open, drinking the water poured by Aquarius above it.

Pavo

Of the 12 bird constellations, Pavo (PAY-vo), the peacock, is a southern one, along with Grus, Tucana, and Phoenix. It is best seen on July evenings, spreading its tail feathers across the southern skies. This large constellation stretches across almost a twelfth of the width of the night sky.

Pavo represents the peacock belonging to the Greek goddess Hera, which pulled her heavenly chariot.

Peacock

Its stars appear to spread out like the feathers in a peacock's tail.

Nu Octantis 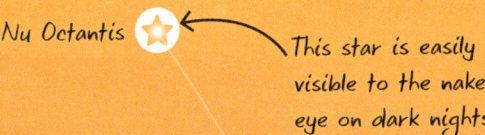 ← This star is easily visible to the naked eye on dark nights.

Its three stars make a nearly triangular shape.

Octans

Nicolas Louis de Lacaille named Octans (OCK-tanz) after a navigational instrument, the octant, in the 18th century. Octans lies at the south celestial pole, so it never goes below the horizon when seen from the southern hemisphere. Though this dim constellation is visible throughout the year, it's best seen in October.

Octants were used to find the position of stars before the invention of sextants.

Ionnina

Most of its stars form a thin, diamond-like shape.

Johannes Hevelius originally named it Sobieski's Shield, in honour of John III Sobieski, a Polish King.

Scutum

The fifth-smallest constellation, Scutum (SCYOOT-um), the shield, lies close to the centre of the Milky Way. While its outline has only six dim stars, Scutum is easy to spot on a dark night thanks to the star-filled sky around it. It can be seen from most parts of the world, and the best month to look for it is August.

Telescopium

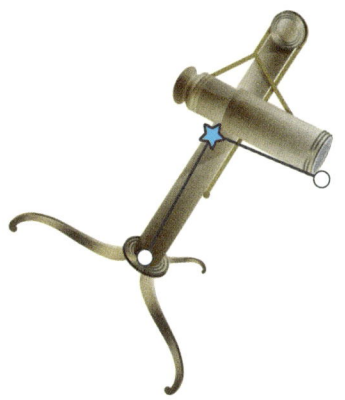

In the 1700s, Lacaille listed 14 constellations in the southern sky, and Telescopium (teh-lih-SKO-pi-um) was one of them. He first called it Tubus Astronomicus after an old telescope used at the Paris Observatory at that time. On August evenings, look for this tiny constellation hanging close to the Teapot in Sagittarrius and the tail of Scorpius.

Once much larger, Telescopium was reduced in size by the Belgian astronomer Eugène Delport in 1930.

Alpha Telescopii

This star is 800 times brighter than the Sun.

This star sits near the base of the telescope.

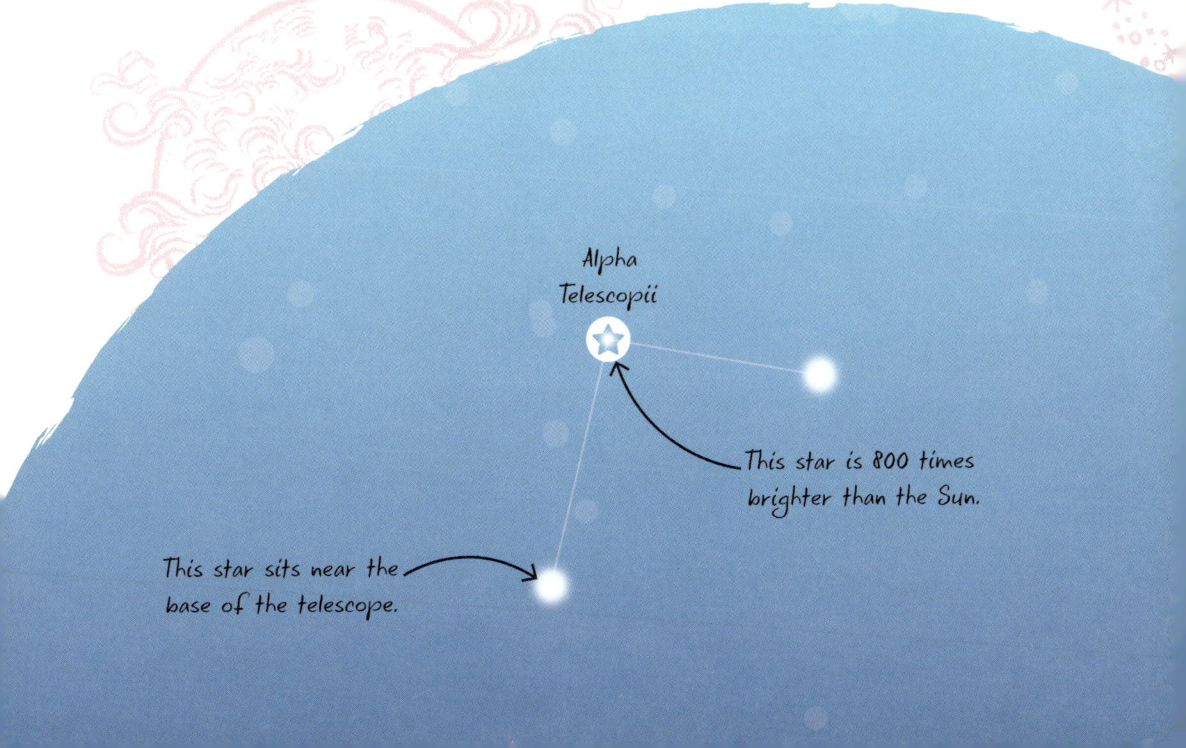

Tucana

Best known for the Small Magellanic Cloud, Tucana (tu-CA-na) has no bright stars. It is located near the south celestial pole and is most visible in October. This starry toucan is a southern circumpolar constellation, meaning it never sets when viewed from the southern hemisphere.

Some early Dutch astronomers thought Tucana resembled a hornbill instead, because of its similar-shaped beak.

Toucan's beak

 Alpha Tucanae

This line represents a branch with a berry, hanging from the toucan's beak.

Zodiacal constellations

There are 12 constellations in the night sky associated with the star signs of the western zodiac. These are called zodiacal constellations. They sit in a special band in the sky called the zodiac, which is an imaginary belt around the Earth. In astrology, these constellations are special because the Sun passes through them. Your star sign is the one the Sun was crossing when you were born. In astronomy, these constellations are just as important and fascinating as any other star patterns in the sky.

The ecliptic

The Sun's imaginary path across the sky is called the ecliptic. From Earth, it looks as if the Sun slowly moves across the sky. But it's actually the Earth that travels around the Sun in an orbit. This journey takes one year, while the Sun stays fixed.

Planets

All planets in the Solar System orbit the Sun, forming a flat, disc-like shape around it. So, when the Sun appears to move along the ecliptic, the seven planets seem to follow it, too.

Zodiac

Throughout the year, the Sun appears to move across a band of constellations that lie along the ecliptic. This band is called the zodiac. When we say the Sun is "in" a zodiac sign, it means it is in front of that zodiacal constellation in the sky.

Moon

The Moon's orbit is at a different angle from the ecliptic. If they lined up perfectly, there would be a lunar and a solar eclipse every month. However, when eclipses do happen, the Moon crosses the ecliptic.

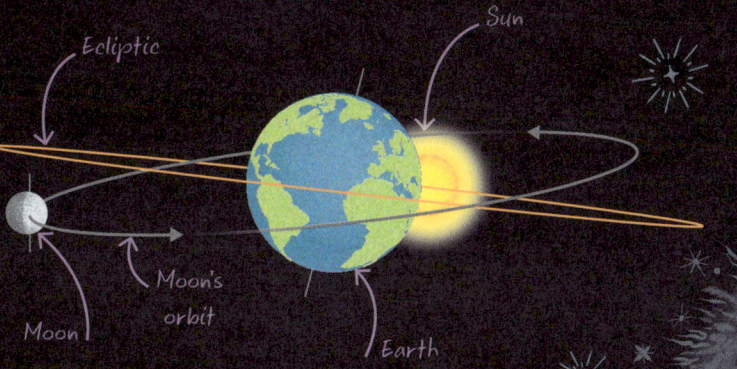

How to find the ecliptic

If there are planets visible in the night sky, you can easily trace the ecliptic. For instance, look for Venus and Mercury in the sunset sky. Trace a line across them and the setting Sun on the horizon. This line will loosely follow the path of the ecliptic on the celestial sphere. Knowing where the ecliptic is, you can easily find many other celestial objects.

The ecliptic is tilted like the Earth.

Capricornus

First noted by Ptolemy, Capricornus (cap-rih-CORN-us) is the smallest and one of the dimmest zodiacal constellations. Ancient astronomers saw it as a goat with the tail of a fish. They also associated it with the winter solstice — the shortest day and longest night of the year in the northern hemisphere. This faint "sea goat" can be best spotted in September evenings.

The ancient Greeks saw Capricornus as the goat-like god Pan, who grew a fish's tail to escape from the monster Typhon.

This star sits in the fish's tail.

Deneb Algedi

Its outline creates an arrowhead or a nearly triangular shape.

Sadalsuud

← This odd shape made by the stars depicts the water poured from the cup.

Aquarius

Most visible in October, Aquarius (uh-KWARE-ree-us), the water bearer, swims near other water constellations. This well-known group of stars is associated with many mythologies. It represented the water god Ea for the Babylonians, while Egyptians saw it as the god of the Nile.

Greeks associated Aquarius with Ganymede, the son of Tros, who was made to hold a cup of water for the gods.

Pisces

Pisces (PAI-seez) is a faint but significant constellation most clearly seen in November. It contains the point where the Sun crosses the Earth's equator while moving south to north. This event is called the March equinox. To locate Pisces, look for the star pattern Circlet that sits on the head of the western fish (right). Then move towards the leaping eastern fish (left).

In Roman mythology, the fishes of Pisces were Venus and Cupid, who tied themselves together to flee from a sea monster.

Pisces can also be identified by the V shape its stars make.

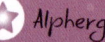 Alpherg

Circlet

To find Aries, look for these three stars arranged in an arc.

Hamal
Sheratan
Mesarthim

With its head turned back towards its body, it seems as if the ram is admiring its golden fleece.

Aries

The stars of Aries (AY-reez) are not very bright, so the best time to look for this zodiacal constellation is on a dark December night. In Greek mythology, it represented the mythical ram with a golden fleece. The Egyptians associated it with their god Amon, who had the body of a human and the head of a ram.

Almost triangle-shaped pattern of stars at the back

These stars form a backwards question mark called the Sickle.

Leo Triplet

Regulus

Leo represents the notorious lion of Nemea that was later killed by Hercules, a Greek hero.

Leo

High in the night sky, Leo (LEE-oh), the lion, prowls among the stars. It is home to the famous Leo Triplet — a group of three interconnected galaxies — and the Leonid meteor shower, which peaks in late November. This starry king is most visible in April from both hemispheres, watching over the world.

Virgo

Resting between Leo and Libra, Virgo (VER-go), the maiden, is the second-largest constellation and the largest in the zodiac. It holds thousands of galaxies, including the Sombrero Galaxy, which is shaped like a sombrero or Mexican sun hat. Spot Virgo on late May evenings by looking for its brightest star, Spica.

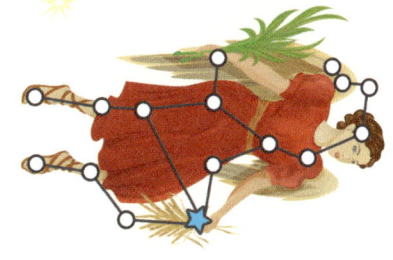

In many cultures, Virgo is seen as the goddess of harvest, holding a bunch of wheat.

It makes a closed shape in the centre, with lines almost like arms stretching from each corner.

Spica

Sombrero Galaxy

Scorpius

Scorpius (SCOR-pee-us) slinks across the southern sky — its stinger raised and tail curling behind. At its heart lies Antares, a fiery star so red it's often called a rival of the red planet Mars. This summertime constellation is visible worldwide, but best seen in July in the southern hemisphere, where it sits higher in the sky.

A myth says that Scorpius stung Orion to death, so when Scorpius rises in the sky, Orion sets.

Antares

To spot Scorpius, look for the capital "J" shape in the sky.

The tail of Scorpius forms a star pattern called the fish hook.

Under a telescope, the Beehive Cluster looks like a swarm of bees.

Al Tarf

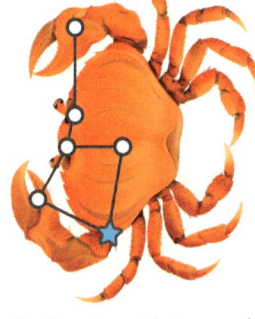

In Greek mythology, when Heracles kicked Cancer, the crab, into the sky, Hera placed it among the stars.

Cancer

Appearing the faintest in the sky, Cancer (CAN-ser) is actually home to many dazzling deep-sky objects. It includes the Beehive Cluster, which is one of the closest open star clusters to the Solar System. Although Cancer is widely imagined as a crab, ancient Egyptians saw a dung beetle in its shape. Stargazers around the world watch out for this crab on March evenings.

Libra

Hanging below the celestial equator, Libra (LEE-bruh) is the only zodiacal constellation that does not represent a living thing. Early Greek astronomers considered it part of Scorpius, but the Romans later separated this dim group of stars. Watch the scales of Libra rising high in the southern skies in June.

Romans called this constellation "balance", as it includes the autumn equinox.

Zubeneschamali

Libra forms a triangle with two lines hanging from two of its corners.

The Greeks saw the star Zubenelgenubi as the southern claw of Scorpius.

This star, Castor, is actually a family of six stars.

Pollux

The star Propus grows and shrinks over time, creating a throbbing effect in the sky.

Greek sailors regarded the twin brothers, Castor and Pollux, as their guardians at sea.

Gemini

Find the Gemini (jeh-mee-NAI) twins in the night sky by looking for two dazzling stars sitting next to each other — Pollux and Castor. The stars in this constellation create an outline of two people holding hands, with the twin stars as the heads. Catch a glimpse of Gemini in the northern skies during winters, and in February from the rest of the world.

All stars in Pleiades are born from the same cloud of gas and dust.

Aldebaran

This V-shaped group of stars is called the Hyades.

Taurus

Sitting next to Orion, this zodiacal constellation is one of the easiest to recognize in the night sky. Taurus (TOR-us) contains two shiny star clusters, the Pleiades and the Hyades. The constellation is visible from all over the world, and the best time to view this cosmic bull is in January.

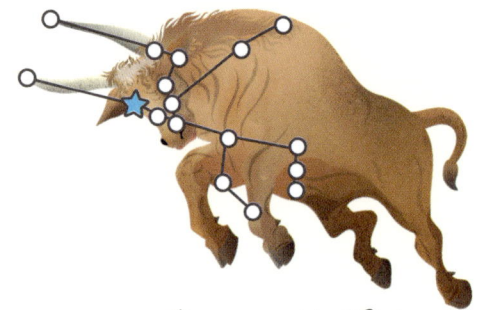

Taurus was identified by ancient astronomers at least 2,500 years ago.

Sagittarius

One of the largest constellations, Sagittarius (sah-juh-TARE-ee-us) aims its glowing bow across the southern sky. Watch this cosmic archer shine high on clear August evenings. At its heart is the Teapot asterism, a group of stars many stargazers use to find the constellation. It is also home to Sagitarrius A* — a supermassive black hole at the centre of the Milky Way.

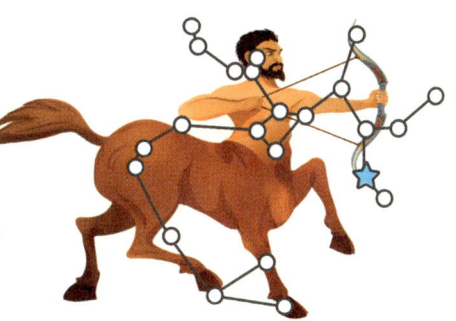

People from the ancient city of Sumer (now in southern Egypt) pictured it as a figure with the lower body of a horse.

This star marks the top of the archer's bow.

This sits in the hindleg of the creature.

⭐ Kaus Australis

Rasalhague — Head of the god

Its central stars form an outline of a house.

The depiction of the Greek god of medicine holding a snake is a traditional symbol for healing.

Ophiuchus

One of the biggest constellations, Ophiuchus (off-ee-YOO-kus) is sometimes counted as the 13th zodiac sign because it sits along the ecliptic. It represents the Greek god of medicine, holding the neighbouring Serpens. The serpent bearer stands high in the southern skies and is most visible in July.

Stargazing tips

You can watch stars from your window. But if you'd like to make stargazing even more enjoyable, here are some helpful ideas.

Choose a location

For the best stargazing experience, find areas with little light pollution. Places like a big park, far from street lights, or on top of buildings can be good spots to observe fainter stars and constellations.

Check the weather

The best weather for stargazing is a clear night, without any clouds in the sky. Check the weather ahead of time to plan your stargazing night and prepare accordingly.

Use a red light torch

It takes about 20–45 minutes for your eyes to fully adjust to the dark. In case you need extra light, use a dim red LED light torch. This will not disrupt your night vision as much as other colours do.

Visit an observatory

Many observatories offer stargazing sessions to help people explore the stars. You can also visit planetariums that recreate the night sky indoors.

Careers in stargazing

Stargazing usually refers to the hobby of looking at stars, but it can be much more. You can study different fields to explore space and beyond. Let's look at some of them and the famous experts who led the way in these areas.

Astronomer

Astronomers are scientists who study space objects, including stars. A famous Indian astronomer, Vikram Sarabhai began the country's space program, which led to the creation of the Indian Space Research Organization (ISRO).

Sarabhai is also credited for developing India's space rocket technology.

Astrophysicist

These scientists use physics and maths to understand how stars, planets, and galaxies work. Jocelyn Bell Burnell, a British astrophysicist, discovered pulsars. These are spinning stars that have become an important cosmic tool in studying the Universe, helping with matters such as measuring the distance to a star.

Instrument Systems Manager

These scientists ensure complex instruments like big telescopes work properly during space missions. American scientist Olivia Lupie helps maintain NASA's Hubble Space Telescope so it can keep exploring stars year after year.

Space engineer

Space engineers design and build many instruments for space exploration, such as rockets and satellites. Mary Jackson, an African-American aerospace engineer at NASA, worked on the Apollo 11 mission that sent the first people to the Moon.

Cosmologist

Cosmologists generally study the Universe on a larger scale than astrophysicists. They are interested in how the Universe came into existence and how far galaxies are spread across it. American cosmologist and astronomer Carl Sagan also explored the possibility of life on other planets.

Glossary

amateur astronomy
Activity of studying stars and other celestial objects; also called stargazing

asterism
Pattern of stars that is not officially recognized as a constellation by the International Astronomical Union (IAU)

astrology
Field of study that uses the movement of celestial objects to predict future events

astronomy
Scientific study of stars, galaxies, and other objects in space

astrophysicist
Scientist who studies the nature of celestial objects

binary stars
Two stars that orbit each other, held together by gravity

black hole
Region of space with such strong gravity that even light cannot escape

celestial coordinates
Set of numbers used to define the location of an object on the celestial sphere

celestial equator
Imaginary circle around the celestial sphere, directly over the Earth's equator; also the celestial equivalent of the Earth's equator

celestial event
Something that happens because of the interaction of celestial objects

celestial hemispheres
Upper and lower halves of the celestial sphere

celestial object
Object in space, such as stars, planets, and moons

celestial poles
Celestial equivalent of the Earth's North and South Poles, around which the celestial sphere seems to turn every day

celestial sphere
Imaginary sphere around the Earth, on which stars and other celestial objects appear to lie

cosmologist
Scientist who studies the origin and nature of the Universe

cosmos
All of the Universe and everything it contains

deep-sky object
Celestial object outside our Solar System, including galaxies, nebulae, and star clusters, but not individual stars

dwarf star
Small-sized star, low in brightness

Earth's axis
Imaginary line around which the Earth spins; it runs through the middle of the planet, from the North Pole to the South Pole

eclipse
This occurs when an object in space passes into the shadow of another object. A solar eclipse happens when the Moon's shadow is cast on Earth. During a lunar eclipse, the Earth's shadow is cast on the Moon

ecliptic
Imaginary path the Sun follows across the sky

equinox
Time of year when the Sun crosses the celestial equator, making the day and night almost the same length

galactic poles
Refer to both north and south poles of a galaxy

galaxy
Huge group of stars, gas, and dust in space, held together by gravity

horizon
Imaginary line in the far distance, where the sky seems to meet the land or sea

International Astronomical Union (IAU)
Organization that studies the Universe; it gives official names to space objects and decides what astronomical terms mean worldwide

latitude
Imaginary line running horizontally around the Earth, above and below the equator

light year
Distance travelled by a beam of light in one year

longitude
Imaginary line running from the North Pole to the South Pole on the Earth

Magellanic Clouds
Small galaxies near the Milky Way; they are called the Large and Small Magellanic Clouds

mass
Amount of matter an object contains

meteor
Streak of light created by dust, gas, or rocks entering the Earth's atmosphere and burning up

meteor shower
Event that occurs when lots of meteors fall together through the Earth's atmosphere

Milky Way
The spiral galaxy that holds our Solar System

naked eye
Refers to seeing something without the help of an equipment, such as a telescope or binoculars

navigation
Finding directions to reach a particular location

nebula
Huge cloud of dust and gas in space

nova
Star that erupts temporarily, increasing brightness by many thousands of times

observatory
Place used for observing the night sky and space events, using special equipment like telescopes

orbit
Path followed by a celestial object around another object in space

planisphere
Flat, circular map of the night sky, used to locate stars and other night-sky objects

Pole Star
Star closest to the north celestial pole, which is often used for navigation; also called Polaris

pulsar
Fast spinning star that gives out regular flashes of light

solstice
Time of year when the Sun is at its highest or lowest point in the sky, making the longest or shortest day

star cluster
Group of stars held together by gravity

star map
Chart that shows where stars and constellations are located in the sky

stargazer
Person who studies or likes to look at stars and other objects in the sky

supergiant
Large star that is hundreds of times the mass of the Sun

supernova
Explosion of a star, for a few weeks or months, which causes the star to shine millions of times more brightly

zodiac
Imaginary belt on the ecliptic that passes through 13 constellations

Index

A
Achernar 62
Albireo 45
Algenib 52
Algol 26
Alpha Centauri A and B 61, 87
Alpha Hydri 65
Alpha Mensae 67
Alpha Pictoris 69
Alpheratz 24, 52
Altair 43, 46, 48, 73
Andromeda 24
Andromeda Galaxy 24, 61
Antares 114
Antlia 74
Antlia Cluster 74
Apollo missions 123
apps 13
Apus 85
Aquarius 109
Aquila 43, 73
Ara 86
Arcturus 34, 60
Argo Navis 76, 80, 83
Aries 111
Arneb 58
asterisms 48–49
astrology 6
astronomers 6–7, 17, 18, 20, 122
astrophysicists 122
Auriga 28
auroras 11, 13
autumn equinox 116

B
Beehive Cluster 115
Bell Burnell, Jocelyn 122
Beta Centauri 61
Beta Equulei 47
Beta Gruis (Tiaki) 96
Beta Pictoris 69
Beta Trianguli 27, 94
Betelgeuse 33
binary stars 15, 53, 68, 81
binoculars 12
black holes 44, 119
blue giants 14
Boötes 34, 60
Brahe, Tycho 17
brightness 21

C
Caelum 56
Camelopardalis 29
Cancer 115
Canes Venatici 36
Canis Major 75
Canis Minor 30
Capella 28
Capricornus 108
Caput Trianguli 27
careers, stargazing 122–123
Carina 76
Carina Nebula 76
Cassiopeia 25, 61
Castor 117
celestial coordinates 19
celestial equator 18
celestial objects 8–9, 21
celestial poles 18
celestial sphere 18–19
Centaurus 61, 87
Cepheus 44
Cetus 57
Chamaeleon 77
Circinus 88
Circlet 110
clouds 121
Columba 59
Coma Berenices 37
compasses 13
computer programs 13
constellations 10–11, 13, 20–21
Corona Australis 95
Corona Borealis 38, 95
Corvus 89
cosmologists 123
Crater 78
Crux 49, 60, 61, 77, 90, 92
Cygnus 45

D
declination 19
deep-sky objects (DSO) 21
Delphinus 46
Delport, Eugène 103
Delta Cephei 44
Delta Sagitta 53
Deneb 45, 48
Deneb el Okab 43
Diphda 57
Dorado 66
Draco 41
Dumbbell Nebula 54
dwarf stars 14

E
Earth, movement of 16–17, 18, 19
Earth-centred Universe 17
eclipses 10, 107
eclipsing binaries 15
ecliptic, the 106–107
Emu 73
equinoxes 110, 116
Equuleus 47
Eridanus 62
eyes, adjusting 121

F
Fomalhaut 99
Fornax 63

G
galaxies 9, 21, 61, 63, 64, 71, 83, 93
Gamma Caeli 56
Gamma Cassiopeia 25
Ganges, River 62
Gemini 117
giant stars 14
globular star clusters 15
gravity 14, 15
Grus 96

H
Habrecht, Isaac II 70
hemispheres, northern and southern 11, 17, 22, 55
Hercules 40
Hevelius, Johannes 7, 31, 32, 36, 82, 102
Horologium 64
Hubble Space Telescope 123
Hyades 118
Hydra 79
Hydrus 65

I
Indian Space Research Organization (ISRO) 122
Indus 97
instrument systems managers 123

J
Jackson, Mary 123
Jewel Box 90
Job's Coffin 46

K
Kitalpha 47
Kochab 42

L
Lacaille, Nicolas Louis de 7, 56, 63, 67, 70, 71, 88, 93, 101, 103
Lacerta 50
Large Magellanic Cloud 66
latitude 19
Leo 112

Leo Minor 31
Leo Triplet 112
Lepus 58
Libra 1, 16
light pollution 121
light years 9
longitude 19
lunar eclipses 10, 107
Lupie, Olivia 123
Lupus 91
Lynx 32
Lyra 51, 73

M

magnitude 21
March equinox 110
Markab 52
Mars 114
mass 44
Mensa 67
Mercury 107
meteor showers 8, 9, 13, 51, 112
Microscopium 98
Milky Way 9, 21, 43, 49, 50, 53, 55, 66, 73, 80, 93, 102, 119
Mira 57
Mirfak 26
Monoceros 33
Moon 10, 107
moons 8
Musca 92
myths and legends 20, 72–73

N

NASA 123
navigation 7, 81
nebulae 14, 21, 43
Norma 93
North Star 17, 48
northern constellations 22–54
Northern Cross 45
northern lights 11
novae 81

O

observatories 121
Octans 101
Omega Centauri 87
open star clusters 15, 115
Ophiuchus 39, 120
orbits 16, 106–107
Orion 23, 72
Orion Nebula 23

P

Pavo 100
Pegasus 52
Perseus 26
Phact 59

Phekad 42
Phoenicians 7
Phoenix 68
Pictor 69
Pisces 110
Piscis Austrinus 99
Plancius, Petrus 29, 59, 77, 97
planetariums 121
planetary motion 16
planets 106, 107
planispheres 19
Pleiades 15, 118
Plough (Big Dipper) 35, 48, 60, 72
Polaris 11, 42, 60
Pollux 117
Praecipua 31
Procyon 30, 33
Propus 117
Proxima Centauri 9, 87
Ptolemy, Claudius 6, 20, 51, 75, 86, 91, 108
pulsars 122
Puppis 80
Pyxis 81

R

red supergiants 14
Reticulum 70
right ascension 19
rotation of Earth 16–17, 18, 19

S

Sagan, Carl 123
Sagitta 53
Sagittarius 119
Sagittarius A* 119
Sarabhai, Vikram 122
Scheat 52
Schedar 25
Scorpius 73, 114
Sculptor 71
Scutum 102
Segin 25
Serpens 39
Serpens Caput 39
Serpens Cauda 39
Sextans 82
Sickle 112
Sirius 33, 75
Small Magellanic Cloud 104
solar eclipses 10, 107
solstices 108
Sombrero Galaxy 113
south celestial pole 17, 77, 83, 90, 101, 104
South Galactic Pole 71
southern constellations 55–104
Southern Cross see Crux
southern lights 11
space engineers 123
Spica 113

Spindle Galaxy 82
star birth 14
star charts 7
star clusters 15, 21, 43, 63
star death 14, 15, 58
star hopping 60–61
star trails 17
stargazing 6–7, 121
stars 8, 14–15
Summer Triangle 43, 46, 47, 48, 54
Sun 7, 8, 17, 106–107
Sun-centred Universe 17, 106
supergiants 14
supermassive black holes 119
supernovae 15

T

Taurus 118
Teapot 49, 103, 119
Teaspoon 49
telescopes 12–13
Telescopium 103
Thuban 41
torches, red light 121
Triangulum 27
Triangulum Australe 61, 88, 94
Tucana 104

U

Ursa Major 10, 35, 48, 60
Ursa Minor 42

V

Varahamihira 6
variable stars 15
Vega 40, 48, 73
Vela 83
Vela Supercluster 83
Venus 107
Virgo 113
Volans 84
Vulpecula 54

W

weather 121
Whirlpool Galaxy 36
white dwarfs 14, 15
Winter Hexagon 49
winter solstice 108
Winter Triangle 30

X

Xu 47

Z

Zeta Phoenicis 68
Zhang Heng 6
Zodiac 105, 106
zodiacal constellations 105–119
Zubenelgenubi 116

Senior editor Kritika Gupta
Editor Syed Tuba Javed
Senior art editors Vikas Chauhan, Kanika Kalra
Art editors Prateek Maurya, Mohd Zishan
Pre-production designers Rakesh Kumar, Dheeraj Singh
Pre-production image editor Nityanand Kumar
Senior picture researcher Nishwan Rasool
Senior jacket designer Rashika Kachroo
Managing editor Roohi Sehgal
Managing art editors Diane Peyton Jones, Ivy Sengupta
Associate publisher Gemma Farr
Production editor Gillian Reid
Production controller John Casey
Delhi creative head Malavika Talukder
Art director Mabel Chan

Editorial consultant Phil Hunt

First published in Great Britain in 2025 by
Dorling Kindersley Limited
20 Vauxhall Bridge Road,
London SW1V 2SA

The authorised representative in the EEA is
Dorling Kindersley Verlag GmbH. Arnulfstr. 124,
80636 Munich, Germany

Copyright © 2025 Dorling Kindersley Limited
A Penguin Random House Company
10 9 8 7 6 5 4 3 2 1
001–351126–Dec/2025

All rights reserved.
No part of this publication may be reproduced, stored in or introduced into a retrieval system, or transmitted, in any form, or by any means (electronic, mechanical, photocopying, recording, or otherwise), without the prior written permission of the copyright owner.
DK values and supports copyright. Thank you for respecting intellectual property laws by not reproducing, scanning or distributing any part of this publication by any means without permission. By purchasing an authorised edition, you are supporting writers and artists and enabling DK to continue to publish books that inform and inspire readers.
No part of this publication may be used or reproduced in any manner for the purpose of training artificial intelligence technologies or systems. In accordance with Article 4(3) of the DSM Directive 2019/790, DK expressly reserves this work from the text and data mining exception.

A CIP catalogue record for this book
is available from the British Library.
ISBN: 978-0-2417-5983-7

Printed and bound in China

www.dk.com

This book was made with Forest Stewardship Council™ certified paper – one small step in DK's commitment to a sustainable future. Learn more at www.dk.com/uk/information/sustainability

The publisher would like to thank the following for their kind permission to reproduce their photographs: (Key: a-above; b-below/bottom; c-centre; f-far; l-left; r-right; t-top)
2 Dreamstime.com: Denys Bilytskyi. **6 Alamy Stock Photo:** Dinodia Photos RM (cl); Heritage Image Partnership Ltd / © Fine Art Images (bc). **Shutterstock.com:** Triston Tan (br). **7 Alamy Stock Photo:** Heritage Image Partnership Ltd / © Fine Art Images (ca); Lanmas (bl). **Dreamstime.com:** Tanialerro (b/Watercolor Texture). **8 Dreamstime.com:** Kevin Carden (tl); Wirestock (cl). **9 Alamy Stock Photo:** B.A.E. Inc. (cl); Jamie Pham (tr). **Dreamstime.com:** Mhmihmai (br); Tanialerro (b/Watercolor Texture). **10–11 Dreamstime.com:** Rastan (b). **11 Dreamstime.com:** Mumemories (tl); Tanialerro (t/Watercolor Texture). **Shutterstock.com:** PlanilAstro (br). **12 Dreamstime.com:** Weber11 (cl). **12–13 Dreamstime.com:** Seonlockephotography (b). **13 Dreamstime.com:** Mikhail Kokhanchikov (cra). **Shutterstock.com:** New Africa (crb). **14 Depositphotos Inc:** Blueringmedia (cr). **Dreamstime.com:** Markus Schieder (bl); Tanialerro (cr/Watercolor Texture). **15 Dreamstime.com:** Corey A Ford (bl); Kom Vitthayanukarun (cr); Tanialerro (b/Watercolor Texture). **Getty Images / iStock:** E+ / Manfred_Konrad (tl). **16 Dreamstime.com:** Olga Kurbatova (r). **17 Alamy Stock Photo:** Heritage Image Partnership Ltd / Historica Graphica Collection (br). **Dreamstime.com:** Tanialerro (b/Watercolor Texture). **Getty Images / iStock:** Abriendomundo (tl). **19 Dreamstime.com:** Tanialerro (r/Watercolor Texture). **20 Alamy Stock Photo:** Charles Walker Collection (cr). **21 Dreamstime.com:** Tanialerro (br/Watercolor Texture). **Getty Images / iStock:** Brightstars (tl). **NASA:** The Hubble Heritage Team (STScI / AURA) (cr). **61 Dreamstime.com:** Tanialerro (t/Watercolor Texture). **72 Alamy Stock Photo:** Historic Collection (br); Pictures Now (cl). **73 Alamy Stock Photo:** VWPics / Alan Dyer (tr). **Dreamstime.com:** Tanialerro (tr/Watercolor Texture). **121 Dreamstime.com:** Anatolyigleb (cla); Anmbph (cr); Tanialerro (cla/Watercolor Texture, b/Watercolor Texture). **Getty Images:** Moment / Michael Orso (tl). **122 Dreamstime.com:** Tanialerro (br/Watercolor Texture). **Getty Images:** Corbis Entertainment / Colin McPherson (br); Hulton Archive / Dinodia Photos (cl). **123 Alamy Stock Photo:** NASA Image Collection (cl); NASA Photo (br). **NASA:** NASAs Goddard Space Flight Center / Bill Hrybyk (tr)

About the author:
Abigail Beall is a science journalist popular for her monthly column, Stargazing at Home, in *New Scientist*. With her expertise in physics, astronomy, and cosmology, Abigail has also authored many amazing books on urban astronomy.

DK would like to thank:
Soumya Rampal for editorial support; Nidhi Mehra and Roohi Rais for design support; Samrajkumar S and Sakshi Saluja for picture research assistance; Jonathan Melmoth for proofreading; Helen Peters for the index; Mohd Zishan for main constellations and additional illustrations.

From the author:
A huge thank you to my husband Joel for the discussions, ideas, and support while I worked on this book. To Mum, Dad, Gus, Hilary, and Stewart for all of their help. To my son, Rowan, who is my biggest (and newest) inspiration.